W. J. GRUFFYDD

1881–1954

Photograph by Dafydd Gruffydd

T. J. Morgan

W. J.

GRUFFYDD

University of Wales Press
on behalf of the Welsh Arts Council

1970

I well remember a review by Mr. St John Ervine of a book of criticism of a certain playwright, in which the critic was given a real drubbing for not coming down occasionally from the heights of pure interpretation to give the reader a few useful biographical facts, such as the date of birth. William John Gruffydd was born on February 14, 1881 in the village of Bethel, which is within the parish of Llanddeiniolen in Caernarvonshire. He was the eldest son of John and Jane Elizabeth Griffith. There is some significance in the spelling of the surname. The correct Welsh spelling is Gruffudd, with Gruffydd as a variant. 'Griffith' is the closest approximation in an English spelling system. Most Welsh people bearing the surname had succumbed without protest to the conventional English spelling and in most parts of Wales with the English s , Griffiths. Going back to the Welsh form of Gruffydd is indicative not so much of a desire to restore the correct form for the sake of accuracy, as of an insistence on Welshness and even of a spirit of truculence. And as I am extracting meanings out of names, it is worth noting that John Griffith's eldest brother had the surname of Jones. The grandfather's christian

1

name was John, and as late as 1840 in this remote area, there still survived this older Welsh method of naming which turned the father's christian name into the son's surname—only in the case of the eldest son in this instance.

Bethel was more than a hamlet but these slate quarrying villages, compared to the bustling jungles of habitation in the mining villages of Glamorgan, would regard themselves as rural. Many of the householders would have a tract of grazing land, very poor land it is true, but sufficient to keep one or two cows and to give to many a quarryman's life a touch of the crofter's existence. This may have added a little means of subsistence to the quarryman's scanty earnings, but it certainly added also to his work and worry. Everything one reads, in the form of biography or fiction, makes one realise what a terribly hard life it was. They wanted very little out of life and they were content if they could scrape a living and keep out of debt; there was never a thought of any treat or holiday for one's self; it wasn't right for that sort of relaxation to be taken by the peasantry: their satisfaction (apart from religious consolations and spiritual reward) was to save enough so as eventually to own their house and, may be, to send son or daughter to college or to enable them to get a better start in life than they themselves had had. Here was a peasantry just beginning to emerge from the subjugation of poverty and from social and political insignificance, quite prepared to do without the fruits of their labours provided their children would benefit—prepared even to work their fingers to the bone and to rival an anchorite in self-denial.

The young, sensitive, sympathetic poet when he
matured sufficiently to assess the sacrificial
quality of this form of existence could not fail
to be moved by its rewardlessness. However
rebellious a young intellectual might be in his
attitude to and criticism of the narrowness and
self-righteousness and censoriousness of his
people's religion, he saw that charity and decency
and neighbourliness emanated naturally from
their hearts. It may be a complete misuse of
psychological jargon, but the words 'love-hate
relationship' were as if specially devised to
describe Gruffydd's attitude to the chapel-going
peasantry of his home and village and
upbringing,—or rather, his varying attitudes,
for he was a man of moods, one day in black
despair and the next bubbling over with joy.
When I wrote the essay for the memorial number
of Y LLENOR I tried to describe Gruffydd's
temperament by suggesting, although I had
never in fact seen one, that it was like a seismo-
graph in the way it was affected by the slightest
tremors which would leave the rest of us quite
unmoved and unaffected. Sir Emrys Evans,
having known him well and seen his outbursts
in committee and in writings, remarked to me
that nothing could be more apt to convey the
temperamental extremes of Gruffydd's nature.
There are times when I think I need the
connotations of all the medieval humours to
account for his variability, sanguine, splenetic,
and so on; and I am making this point at an early
stage in this essay for I have already had cause,
right at the start, to mention 'love-hate
relationship'. Inconsistency is the wrong word;
the symbol one needs to have in mind is the

outline of a range of peaks; one wouldn't say the peak is inconsistent with the trough or *cwm;* one is up and the other is down.

In an essay intended for readers not familiar with Welsh literature and knowing little maybe about Welsh history, I feel something should be said about the significance of the name of the village, Bethel, and the name of the parish, Llanddeiniol-en, for they play a great part in Gruffydd's writing and the traditions of which they are symbols need to be understood. Needless to say, the name of the church and its parish was an ancient one; the name of the village was of recent origin. Many of the older church parishes in Wales covered vast areas, especially in mountainous and moorland country with only a sprinkling of population, in scattered farms. When any industrial development in the nine-teenth century, such as the quarrying of slate in Caernarvonshire, brought little clusters of habitations into existence in places that were chosen because of their convenience to the quarry, the clusters became separate communities and there might be three or four communities within the area of the original ecclesiastical parish, needing address-names of their own; they couldn't all be given the original parish name, and in many instances, this would not be appropriate for the original church and its own little cluster of houses, if any, would be a considerable distance away and be another place. It was inevitable therefore that these new communities should be given a new name whenever the older name had become inappropriate because of remoteness from the parish church, and whenever the size of the new community justified a separate address. To take examples from the history of industrial development in South Wales: Morriston needed a new name, within the parish of Llangyfelach; Pontardawe is a new name, within the parish of Llan-giwg. It often happened that the only notable structure in the community of recent growth was the nonconformist chapel and it was inevitable, unless there was a bridge or road-junction already there, that the chapel's name should become the recognised address name; hence Bethel and Carmel and Nebo and Bethesda.

Periodic outbreaks of religious revivals would have brought the majority of the population into the various nonconformist folds, Calvinistic Methodist, Wesleyan Methodist, Baptist, or Congregational—or Independent, for, in Welsh, we use this name with its origins in early and especially Cromwellian Puritanism for the denomination that is called Congregational. It had become normal to be chapel-going. There was a remnant of unconverted people, a few churchgoers and the others just pagans of indifference, and in the eyes of the self-righteous nonconformists, these two classes would be more or less the same. The English-speaking landowner class or squirearchy would be church-going, and their retainers, of course, gamekeeper or coachman; and there might be in the slate-quarrying community an occasional lick-spittle sort of works-bos; or foreman who would deliberately choose to be stuck-up and church-going to please the owners. The speech of Arvon evolved the noun *cynffonnwr* for this type; it is derived from *cynffon* meaning 'tail' (of animal) and the contemptuous meaning of the verb *cynffonna* and the noun *cynffonnwr*, comes from the tail-wagging of the dog, playing up to its owner and wanting to be friendly and patted and petted. It might be proper for a self-respecting nonconformist worker to be civil to the land-owner and quarryowner, but not to be tail-wagging for smiles and favours. In that relationship, between landowner and quarry-owner and their tenants and workmen there was cold civility, if not open enmity, for one side was English-speaking and anglican and the other was Welsh-speaking and nonconformist, and added to this estrangement was the difference of political allegiance, in parliamentary elections and in local matters such as school boards.

The nonconformist or free-church denominat-ions were all the same in the very obvious sense that they had come away at varying times from the established church. They differed from each other in origins and traditions and church government and theology and practice; if they didn't they wouldn't be separate denominations. But although they had by no means become fused by any ecumenical moves, they had influenced each other to such an extent that there was such a thing as Welsh nonconformity, in a positive sense, or Welsh evangelicism, in the nature of the services and the weeknight meetings for prayer and discussion, the fervent style of preaching, family prayers, the Sunday school and the tremendous value placed upon scripture reading and biblical exegesis. If there was a revival it affected all denominations. It is not my task to explain why a certain denomination should be predominant in a given area; or why in certain areas there should be three or possibly four denominations as if in competition. The point I am trying to reach is that Bethel—that is, the chapel that gave its name to the village—was 'Independent'; and despite what has just been said above about the evangelicism and puritanism that were common to all nonconformist denominations, the tradition of Welsh Congregationalism which Gruffydd received allowed him a freedom of interpretation and standpoint which he would never have had from the other denominations. It may be argued that Gruffydd would have been Gruffydd whatever the denomination he was born into, and I am prepared to believe that Gruffydd like others gave to the name "Independent" a theological meaning it was never meant to connote; I still think it is important that his denomination was Welsh Independent; the comparative non-existence of formal creed in the tradition of Welsh Congregationalism gave him a freedom of interpretation and an individualism of protestant belief which he would not have got elsewhere and be allowed to remain a recognised member.

This essay is going to be a series of contradictions; a study of contradiction would be a suitable sub-title. In spite of the left-wing protestantism inherent in Welsh Independency and the extreme modernism and individualism which it allowed Gruffydd to express, we must get used to seeing Gruffydd taking sides which one normally regards as the contrary and sometimes, diametrically opposite. The recent growth of small slate-quarrying communities did not change the rural character of Llanddeiniolen very much, and this small-scale industrialism and self-conscious nonconformity did not turn the established church into complete insignificance. Llanddeiniolen still plays a big part in the texture of Gruffydd's early experience and feeling for associations. I turn again to the industrial valleys of South Wales to bring out a contrast. A young man growing up in Treorci would have hardly any awareness of the original Ystrad-dyfodwg, assuming that all things were the same, i.e. that his home-life was staunchly nonconformist; if he grew up in Morriston in a normal non-conformist family, the ancient church of Llangyfelach a mile away on the hill-top would mean very little to him. Little growths like Bethel couldn't overshadow Llanddeiniolen, and the growth was much too recent, for as soon as the young man of imagination started out on the quest for family history to know who his forebears were, he naturally learned with no need to go very far back that most of them were the untheological and unconverted folk who regarded themselves as simple parishioners, their irregular attendance now become regular and permanent beneath the shadow of the great gnarled yew tree. Some of these according to his grandmother, were plain pagans, not self-conscious unbelievers, but hard-drinking, merry-evening pagans. This was no cause for shame; Gruffydd took great delight in this non-puritan constituent in his ancestry and make-up, especially when puritanism was blamed for banishing the harp and ballad and merry interlude and suppressing the gaiety which these stood for.

He did not need to go outside his home to be taught this about his ancestors for his parents lived with his grandparents, his mother's mother and step-father, and his grandmother was his informant. Gruffydd, after a difficult first period, became greatly attached to his grandmother. Part of his description of her is the word *blin* used in a sense that a South Walian finds difficult to define: the dictionary gives 'unpleasant, disagreeable, peevish, petulant' and I feel an average of these meanings is about right. He also says "She was not easy to live with" and my reason for quoting this is that in the next part of the sentence he admits the same thing concerning himself. This was a typical expression of Gruffydd's; I heard it more than once, 'easy to live with' and 'easy to work with'. I think he meant in this context that he could be obstreperous and headstrong and even defiantly unco-operative, insisting that he was in the right and that everybody else was wrong. Although overtly Calvinistic Methodist, having become so not because of conversion or theological conviction but because her husband was C.M., she lacked the piety or sanctimoniousness which people of her age should have assumed and in moments of blunt candour and irritation, would say things that were outrageous and shocked those around her for her utterances showed no respect for the conventional standards of behaviour and thought and judgement unquestioned by the rest. It is easy to forget that I am paraphrasing what Gruffydd says about his grandmother and momentarily to believe I am describing Gruffydd.

One could hastily draw a superficial conclusion from the data of Gruffydd's rebelliousness and the Victorian evangelicism of his home that he must have spent an unhappy childhood, dashing his head against the wall of strict authority. This conclusion would be very wrong indeed. John Griffith was a very devout and faithful deacon who lived and slaved for his family and his chapel. He very naturally brought up his children to be knowledgeable in the scriptures, to attend all the services regularly and to take part in the religious and administrative or social activity of the church according to their age. There was nothing of the tyrannical Victorian father about this placid, reliable man—I ought to find a word meaning ordinary in a favourable light. Gruffydd does describe in his reminiscences a sort of crisis or showdown resulting from an arrangement that his father had made in the chapel for the son, then aged sixteen, to take his turn in a prayer meeting; Gruffydd was so unwilling that he went so far as to pack his bags to leave home. But this is not evidence of the tyrannical Victorian father, it was quite natural for the father, in all innocence, to make this sort of arrangement and to expect his son to co-operate; taking part in weekday services, such as prayer meetings, was a step taken by most young men in their growth as church members; it might have been a trying and slightly embarrassing experience but it passed off generally without much bother; it was young Gruffydd's over-sensitive nature that made a crisis of it; he was probably afraid of making an ass of himself and I have a feeling that he couldn't regard praying as a sort of exercise that one could take lightly, prayer was a very earnest matter and should never be an exhibition of fluency on one's knees.

His childhood was extremely happy and it had no event to give the amateur psychiatrist any scope. In the last portion of the HEN ATGOFION that he wrote, in which he refers to his happy childhood (Y LLENOR XXVII.3, pp. 111–116) he makes a most illuminating comment: only a very rare few are unlucky enough to have suffered during childhood in a way or to an extent that embittered them for the rest of their lives; in fact when people do speak of an unhappy childhood they are probably extending back into childhood a sense of bitterness then afflicting them. He felt sure that it was the way Owen Edwards' mind developed in manhood that transformed his memory of childhood into bitter dislike—I have more or less given a translation of the original text. The reading material which the home contained would be expository handbooks and denominational magazines with goody-goody stories and bio-graphies in those intended for the young. Here again it is easy to exaggerate because one is dealing with a person who later came to be surrounded by books. It is true that the growing mind was deprived of the kind and supply of books which the professional classes regard nowadays as natural in their children's upbringing; but that makes an unfair comparison and judged by peasant standards the standard of literacy in Gruffydd's home, and the opportunity for intellectual development, were far above average. He pokes fun later on at the goody-goody diet of the religious magazines and his satire turns the examples of virtuous living whose biographies he had to read into sanctimonious humbugs; but he had more to read than most boys and girls of his age and social class, and this satire must not be solemnly interpreted as something "psychological" or anything of the sort; he wouldn't have been conscious of deprivation at the time; it was the development of his mind at a later stage that put the idea into his head; and in any case, literary iconoclasm was a trend, if not a cult, and one had to get idols from somewhere if one had to smash. Instead of emphasising the negative side, deprivation, it is far more proper and important to lay stress upon the positive side of the literacy of his home. Gruffydd knew his Bible thoroughly and he retained an intense interest in the religious doctrines and heresies which had been debated so seriously and at such high intellectual level in Welsh nonconformity in all kinds of ways, in books and magazines, in Sunday school discussion classes, in sermon and public dispute and especially in the quarrymen's shelter hut during any break. Gruffydd has been called the last of the nonconformists; dubbing him with this label was meant to dismiss him; it was an absurd nickname and a misuse of words; but because he was so knowledgeable, as an amateur, in theology and doctrine and so conversant with the biblical text he appears to many of us who have been conditioned by a more secular upbringing to belong to an earlier age.

12

By this time Bethel had a school board and a primary school, to teach the children to read English and simple arithmetic and to name all the capes around the whole coastline of Great Britain, and for the first time to enable the occasional very bright boy and girl to pass to the county school. Wales had a special Education Act of its own, passed in 1889, to enable local authorities to build schools that would provide post-primary education called "Intermediate" for those who passed the scholarship examination: this preceded the Act which brought 'secondary' into use, and the schools that followed the 1889 Act became known as "so-and-so county Intermediate". A number of schools of very great importance in the history of Welsh education came into existence by this means; Caernarvon has the distinction of being the very first, and Gruffydd had the distinction of being the first to enter the first county school—and I think that this means that he headed the list of entrants. One need not use up much space to describe the kind of secondary education that Gruffydd received; one can easily surmise that as the curriculum would contain less science than it does today, and less "modern studies" it would naturally give more room to the established and prestige subjects of the older schools, especially Latin and Greek. I heard Gruffydd claim that they learned as much Latin and Greek before leaving the sixth form as they did in a degree course a generation later and this was probably right in respect of 'prose composition', if not in respect of literature.

What I think is of very great importance during

this period in Gruffydd's career and personal experience was the proximity of the sea. During this impressionable period, seeing small ships and sailors was a daily experience and the call of the sea must have got into his very being. It is more than likely that his decision to serve in the Navy when he joined the forces in 1915 was influenced by the attraction of the impressionable years. His experience in the Navy produced no poem that had a briny or nautical quality. The poetry that is connected with the sea, the old sea captain or the old hulk left to be battered and to dis-intergrate, however late in time the period of composition, has its origin in this period even though the superimposed theme of the passage of time obviously comes from the contemplation of the grown man. He used to splutter impatience whenever he read that his YNYS YR HUD showed the influence of Coleridge on his mind: this sort of comment was so superficial and so much out of focus. The poem is an imaginative synthesis of the lure of the sea and the idea which Gruffydd absorbed from his studies of Welsh and Irish legends, the idea of the sojourn in the Underworld during which time all grief was forgotten and the process of ageing completely arrested, a sojourn of eighty years before the spell is broken and a return voyage of disillusionment back to the world of reality and its struggle for bare living and its inexorable and uncheatable processes of ageing and ceasing to be. One can be fairly certain that the episode of the Underworld in the tale of Branwen daughter of Llyr was the motive and *motif* of the poem—when his studies and interpretations had given him an understanding of it, but the

14

setting of the modern adaptation came from the years when the ships and boats of the Menai straits were like mescalin in the young brain.

The poem YNYS YR HUD has a sort of rubric under the title, namely the lines from the Branwen story which describe the period of oblivion: it ought to have a preface as well, in my view, namely the following passage from the chapter of HEN ATGOFION in Y LLENOR XVII.1, pp.6–15, the chapter on the county school:

But when the teachers had turned their backs we would climb over the gate that had been put there to stop us and would catch a glimpse of one of the world's great sights—Menai Straits beneath us stretching from Aber Menai as far as the bend beneath Llanfair-is-y-gaer, with the Isle of Anglesey facing us, shining green in the distance. I have already said I never got as much as I should have done out of the education provided in the school, but the whole emotional world of my being has been tinged by the intimations of the walls of Caernarvon with the tides of Menai lapping their base. A friend remarked to me the other day how much he liked the traditional verse which ended with the words:

'And the waves being lifted over Caernarvon's walls'

and I could not keep back my superior claim that in my memories I possessed a key to the magic realms of the old verse which he knew nothing of. It isn't just fancy or show-off, or sentimentality either that makes me declare with certainty that the thing of greatest importance by far that came my way in Caernarvon school was the experience one afternoon in July 1899 of seeing Anglesey and Menai, whilst standing on the walls of Caernarvon, one of the three visions of my life.

This passage requires no further interpretation, except to say that although Gruffydd himself mentions three experiences which deserved to be called 'visions', it was part of his nature and therefore of his vocabulary and interpretation to have experiences which because of their profound effect on him, he called 'visions' or 'revelations', and these visions became impulses or sources of creative energy. This became a sort of syllogism; this explained things, this profoundly moving experience, and he saw it at work in the lives of others, the vision becoming impulse; this was the definition of creative activity.

Gruffydd sometimes made use of the editorial notes of Y LLENOR to write obituary notices, or appreciations, of certain persons who were literary figures and to whom he had been very closely attached, people such as R. G. Berry, Principal J. H. Davies, Principal Tom Rees. (Some of these were later republished in the volume of essays, Y TRO OLAF AC YSGRIFAU ERAILL). In the appreciation of Sir John Morris-Jones he states that he came under his influence around the year 1898. This means that he was seventeen plus. Morris-Jones by this time had been teaching for five or six years in the University College of North Wales, and although Gruffydd never became a direct pupil he no doubt at the age of seventeen or eighteen was on the *qui-vive* listening for any new influences in the air especially the criticisms in articles and eisteddfodic adjudications or introductions to edited texts, which attacked the complacency of the existing literary order, bad taste, bombastic style, the pose of metaphysical profundity, the attitude of mind that

16

made the composition of poetry far too facile an accomplishment and, of course, the attitude that poetry was meant to serve public morality and was a metrical form of Religious Instruction. This is not meant to be sarcasm on my part: I am trying to convey the spirit of youth wanting to upset the fuddiduddiness of the literary output, which was so unscholarly and Victorian and shallow.

The next chapter of HEN ATGOFION (Y LLENOR xx.2 pp. 63–68) makes the year 1899 out to be "an important year". This was the year when he made the personal acquaintance of R. Silyn Roberts. Silyn took his initial degree at Bangor in that year but the difference in years between him and Gruffydd was far more than one infers; Silyn had worked in the slate quarries before entering College and was now twenty eight; (1871–1930). He was on the way to the Methodist ministry but having been an academic disciple of Morris-Jones he naturally became a literary disciple, and would have been inoculated against the poetic plagues of the period, the long-winded metricizing of biblical story and what was called the 'New Poet' style, which was a fashion of turning any simple narrative or episode of biography into a labyrinth of metaphysical contemplation, the mind being allowed to stray through the maze of musing and moralizing until it came to a halt, and then picking up the tale or biography once more. Silyn would obviously be a medium to pass on the influences of Morris-Jones to young Gruffydd; for however mild a character Silyn might have been in comparison with the aggressive, assertive

Gruffydd, Silyn after all was twenty eight. Silyn used to cycle fifteen miles to Bethel to call on Gruffydd and they would go for long walks together over the mountains and through the countryside, and one of the results of this was the publication in 1900 of a joint volume of lyrics (TELYNEGION, Jarvis and Foster, Bangor).

There may be nothing in it but as Gruffydd states that they rivalled each other in their admiration of Wordsworth, the question does flit across the mind whether the LYRICAL BALLADS was a precedent for the joint publication. There is nothing to show the authorship of the various poems but the biography of Silyn by David Thomas (p.30) lists those written by Silyn. Of the fifty-one original poems, Gruffydd's share is twenty-seven. One would guess that the eleven pieces translated from Heine were by the one who at that time had been nearest to Morris-Jones's influence; Silyn is also responsible for the translation from D. G. Rossetti. The translation from Catullus is Gruffydd's; and so are the verses from Spain. The short preface ends with this sentence: "We humbly present this simple volume to our nation (or people); our main ambition is that it should be a drop in the flood of the new literary life of Wales". They were decidedly aware that things were stirring and that they were enlisting in a new literary movement, and all the signs are here although not to excess— the slight academic superiority of acquaintance with medieval texts and vocabulary, the trans- lations from Heine and Catullus and a complete disregard of the didactic uses of poetry, and not a semblance of the puckered brow of profound

18

philosophizing. A fervent devotee of the later Gruffydd may feel disappointed when he comes upon this youthful poetry; it would be quite silly to be contemptuous of it, but it hasn't the quality of Mozartian precociousness, and the grown-up Gruffydd had no illusions. When he made his own selection for the collection in the Gregynog volume published in 1932, not one of this first publication survived his scrutiny. "There are several poems in the earliest volumes that I can only regard as exercises and although they are of some value to me personally, as milestones in my development, I do not consider that they should be re-printed"—this comes from the short note prefacing the Gregynog volume. He may have taken himself very seriously at eighteen but he looks back with sardonic humour to this period. Anyone who overheard the voices of Silyn and him when out in a rowing boat would have heard lines and sonnets from Keats and Shelley and Wordsworth being spoken with purest Gwynedd diction. When they had recited all they knew from the works of the great English poets, they continued by reciting their own poems and marvelled to think how two poets of such distinction had miraculously come together in a small rowing boat. It is in this paragraph that Gruffydd declares how they both were attached to Wordsworth although at an earlier age Keats had been his particular favourite. The poems are in the typical nineteenth century light or lightweight lyrical mould; they sound like the words of Schubert and Hugo Wolf *lieder,* about unrequited love and seeing objects that bring the past to mind; of being in love with love, and in love with nature. Since the youthful poet was deliberately refusing to draw upon the style and vocabulary of the heavy-going odes of the eisteddfodic kind, there was not a great deal of fairly modern output of lyrical expression and idiom to feed on. Even if a youthful poet is not consciously setting out to model his own poetry on the style of another, and is not deliberately reproducing, he does need to take in the works of others, just as he takes in food and drink into his body. And what one feels about the work of the eighteen year old Gruffydd is a deficiency in his Welsh poetic diet. In fact one sees evidence of the English diet. The effects of the continuing English diet will remain in later work; one will not need a geiger counter to trace Swinburne and Matthew Arnold, but the proportion of food of Welsh origin in the poet's diet will greatly increase, and Gruffydd's own individual style will get stronger and stronger.

This instance of regarding youthful work as first efforts and exercises is not an isolated one, and this too early publication probably influenced Gruffydd's mind later on in such a way that it became an article of belief, that any sensible self-critical poet should treat his early work and eisteddfodic successes as try-out—the favourite phrase was "serving an apprenticeship". I have a feeling that Gruffydd, as he matured, became somewhat sensitive when he recalled the immaturity of his early work, and that he took himself too seriously at this age. This view was made into a general principle, that things produced at an early age were necessarily immature and undeserving of republication; and that chair and crown poems were mere

W. J. GRUFFYDD

evidence of successful apprenticeship. There was a further clause in the articles of belief concerning youthful work and publication, that quite a large number of young men who were brought within the influences of poetry by the mere process of education, felt a creative urge for a short spell and wrote poems of presentable quality, but they did this not because they were truly gifted but because they felt the effervescence of adolescence and early manhood. The effervescence passes off in most cases and the creative urge dies down; but a few, misled by the effervescence, will continue the practice of writing although the inspiration has gone completely. The genuinely gifted will continue to write not because of a habit started during the period of effervescence, but because of an inner certainty that they have something to say or that something is being said through them.

Further on in the chapter of HEN ATGOFION which calls 1899 an important year, Gruffydd describes how, during his youthful wanderings through the unspoilt loneliness of Arvon there developed in him "the feeling for Nature"; and he refers in particular to the prehistoric fort of Dinas Dinorwig which more than any other spot gave him a special feeling of insight. There is such a thing as fashions in emotions and artistic motives and anyone who wants to be very superior can put this feeling down to the fashion of the romantic movement and the cult of communing with nature. I don't doubt the sincerity of this emotion —and on the one occasion that I spent a day or two in the neighbourhood of his home in Gruffydd's company, he took me to the prehistoric fort which had such significance in the development of his self-awareness and personality. Here the impressionable youth, endowed with powerful imagination, would do much of his reading in the warm days of summer and in pensive intervals would experience a feeling of identity with the place itself, and that he was as much a part of the very nature of the place as the tree and the boulder and the sheep; it was the sensation, combined with perception of the kind which mystics feel. To say that such emotions and experiences are subject to fashion, and influenced by literary vogue, does not invalidate them at all; they can be bogus, of course; a charlatan can make out a claim and make the right noises, and that is why the sceptical critic fears that the semi-mystical experience is of literary origin and not original and authentic. There is no litmus paper one may use to test who is genuine and who is bogus; but one can say that Gruffydd's best work, in poetry and prose, flows from this kind of experience as source.

The year 1899 was important for many other reasons. This was the year he went up to Oxford; and there is an event of importance in the narrative to precede the actual admission to Jesus College in October. It may be a fairly normal experience these days for bright boys from peasant homes and backgrounds to go up to Oxford and Cambridge; we are not exactly *blasé* maybe, but we may fail to appreciate how new and bewildering it must have been seventy years ago. Nothing could be more Welsh than the way it was arranged for Gruffydd and a fellow pupil, H. Parry Jones, to be put up by Owen M. Edwards and his wife, when they came up to sit a scholarship examination in Oriel. Owen Edwards was fellow of Lincoln; he was from Llanuwchllyn in Merionethshire; the headmaster of Bethel village school was G. R. Hughes and he, before coming to Bethel, had been headmaster of the village school of Llanuwchllyn; his wife, Kate, was a sister of Elin, Mrs. Owen Edwards, and it was Mrs. Kate Hughes who arranged for the two boys to stay in her sister's home in Clarendon Villas, Oxford. This isn't mere amusing footnote information. This was only the first act of kindness which Gruffydd received from Owen Edwards. Throughout his three years in Oxford he was regularly invited to the house; he was given encouragement, in word and money, so that his loyal attachment to Owen Edwards combined admiration and indebtedness. A long list could be drawn of tributes and appreciative remarks made by Gruffydd at various stages in his later career, quite apart from the poem To the Reformer written in 1910, and the biography (part one). One may infer that Owen Edwards urged the young poet to publish poems in the journal Cymru for he thanks Owen Edwards in the next volume of verse, published in 1906, for permission to re-print. In going back to my notes I find that the visit to Oxford to sit for a scholarship was not his first long trip from home. H. Parry Jones records that three of them, Gruffydd and O. Arthur Evans (the O.A.E. of one of Gruffydd's *in memoriam* poems) and he were taken by the headmaster to London to take the examination of the "Société de Professeurs de Français en Angleterre".

The external factual part of the undergraduate period need not take much time. He did not distinguish himself in classical moderations; did not proceed to *Greats* in Part Two, but chose the recently established English Literature course, and in his Finals he got a 'second'. This essay will not attempt to describe Gruffydd's interests in the field of Celtic scholarship but because of the overlap of his scholarship and creative work, one has to bring in the name of the principal of Jesus, Sir John Rhŷs. Although the work of John Rhŷs in the fields of Celtic mythology and the analysis of legends has been almost entirely superceded, his contributions as a pioneer were of very great value indeed; his work has none of the careful cataloguing quality of the comparative method used by later students of myths and tales but it is full of daring suggestions and fascinating to read for its own sake, if not for its scientific value. Gruffydd picked up his interest in mythology through the influence of Rhŷs and when he became a university teacher it is not surprising to find that the Mabinogion tales and the Arthurian legend should be one of his fields of study and research. Gruffydd, having once come to admire and be loyal to Rhŷs, stuck to his loyalty; and although it has no relevance to his work as a creative writer to mention this, it may be of interest to some readers to know that he was strongly opposed to the tendency of Germanic scholarship to take from Britain or from Wales a good deal of the 'credit' due to them by minimising the contribution made in Britain to the development of the ancient stories.

It is more relevant to speak of the student society established by the generation immediately preceding, the DAFYDD AP GWILYM SOCIETY. The influence of this society is of great importance in the history of the twentieth century literary revival and of the growth of modern Welsh scholarship; it will no doubt receive attention in another publication in this series. All I wish to do here is to answer a question that naturally occurs to the mind, how could a student society of this kind (when one thinks of hundreds of other student societies) be of such importance at this time. Here assembled were some of the ablest boys of their generation, and yet, because of the state of Welsh scholarship and education, having hardly any acquaintance with the Welsh literature of the past; this was the first contact of many of them with Welsh literature; it was in this way that many became aware of their Welsh identity. Gruffydd did not lack acquaintance with Welsh literature and did not need to go to Oxford to be aware of his Welshness, but what has just been said of the influences of the DAFYDD AP GWILYM SOCIETY upon its members can still be applied, with the addition, *a fortiori*.

An English author who at this time was not ancient enough to be a part of the final honours course became a more potent influence in Gruffydd's life as author than any of the prescribed authors, namely Thomas Hardy. He read a great deal of Hardy's novels during this period, and it is suggested by Parry Jones that

Gruffydd's view of Llanddeiniolen has something of Egdon Heath in it. I am convinced that this is sound observation. And the impression that Hardy made upon him lasted. The poem LLEISIAU'R FYNWENT (*The Voices of the Graveyard*) written in Beaumaris in 1905 is an adaptation of Hardy's 'Friends Beyond', or a transposition into the Llanddeiniolen setting. On a much later occasion Gruffydd had cause to name the books which had affected him most in the sense that they had become essentially part of his view of life and of contemplating man's place in society and in the whole universe, amongst his fellow creatures and amidst the impersonal forces all around him. He names Daniel Owen's first novel Y DREFLAN; JÖRN UHL by Gustav Frenssen, and THE MAYOR OF CASTERBRIDGE. When Hardy died, Gruffydd's editorial notes in Y LLENOR took the form of an essay of appreciation, (Y LLENOR VII.1 pp. 1–4), and this must have meant a great deal to him for he included it in the selection which makes up the volume of essays Y TRO OLAF, (1939). No matter if Hardy was by now out of fashion, Gruffydd writes with the warmth of feeling that got into him twenty-five years back. It is worth translating the last parts because here also there is an excellent example of something that was central to Gruffydd's critical outlook, the intense regard for life and the experience of living—something of the meaning that is so difficult to define may come through the translation:

In all his works, there is only one tragedy, one loss. That tragedy is Death, because Death puts an end to everything that is interesting and lovely and comprehensible, namely Life.

26

It is quite possible for life to be so intense as to become painful to bear, but it is infinitely important that it should be lived and put into words. Not Life with a capital L, not the life of the philosophers and scientists, but that life which is within the comprehension and power of description of the artist, the life of people in small towns and villages, the communion* of ordinary people whose minds can be interpreted because their minds are part of the substance of the known world. And Hardy gives readers the impression that he is a pessimist because he writes under the baneful influence of the dreadful thought that every personality that has come into this life will cease. His lamentation does not come about because he cannot believe in an after-life, it would make no difference to him even if he firmly believed in an after-life. He laments because he regards living as incalculably rich, full of beauty and loveliness, and because living in that sense comes to an end once and for all, it doesn't matter whether there is an after-life or not. He sees and feels nature with faculties so sensitive and in such detail that it hurts, the intense experience being so closely felt. His pity for humanity is given for one thing only—it is pity for the dead for they are deprived of communion with nature and deprived of communion with men. To him the one thing that matters greatly is the mystical communion between man and fellow men, and between man and the world around him; the thing called living.

I will not allow the name pessimist to be given to a man who valued living with greater intensity than any other writer probably, in the world's history; and made life to be so beautiful and so wonderful. For one reader, at least, Hardy reproduces the very act of creation—for he made man out of the soil of the earth and transformed the lifeless earth in such a way that it was no shame to feel one's feet trudging deep in its soil and sludgy clay. I don't know exactly what

*Not a mistranslation for community.

name to use to describe such a writer, but it certainly is not the word pessimist.

Many of these sentences are completely meaningless unless one comprehends that they are gropingly trying to convey the intuitive perception of the mystic and the creative artist, who have to use the vocabulary of every day experience to deal with their rare perception; and there is not much point in further construing by using words like the throb of human life or 'essences' for they are just further examples of the same thing.

It helps to complete the picture of the under-graduate to hear the testimony which some of us heard from the lips of his friend and contemporary, the Reverend John Roberts, who delivered the address in the memorial service which was held in Cardiff. During one whole term he made himself a complete nuisance to the college's kitchen staff: he had been converted to vegetarianism; and he stood out, a lone vegetarian, making it extremely difficult for the kitchen to find anything suitable instead of the food which every one else was given. This regimen ended in a pork pie eaten on Bletchley station on the way home at the end of term. One other thing related to this period is a surmise. One takes for granted the difference which three years in Oxford should make to the outlook of an unsophisticated youth from a village in Gwynedd, conditioned by the values of the home and community, Welsh-speaking, nonconformist, peasant; unless one was obtuse or psychologically unfitted, it was bound to have a broadening effect;

and if one could avoid affectation and a swelled-head, this far from peasant society and form of living were bound to give the educable young man a certain degree of poise and urbanity. It may appear odd and paradoxical, but in spite of his radical and at times left-wing attitude, Gruffydd would take sides with the Anglican church in Wales and be on his own in a Nonconformist camp opposed to the campaign for disestablishing the church; he could get on the most friendly terms with the squire of Greenmeadow and have a sympathetic under-standing of the mental habits of the landed gentry although the instinctive reaction was to regard them as alien and parasitic. As one got inured to the anglican atmosphere of Oxford, the inevitable hostility to the church which was so normal at home, did not look a bit normal in Oxford; especially to a man who by nature sympathised with bottom dogs and minorities and with anybody persecuted by a howling mob or jeering majority. No matter what his own religious views might be, he made tolerance an article of his creed and learnt to be tolerant of everything except intolerance; and I have a feeling that reconciling the views of his condi-tioning at home and the atmosphere of Oxford had much to do with this divesting of prejudice and, of course, the enlightened liberalism of the late nineteenth century. I hope to deal more fully later on with this liberalism of mind, which combines belief and scepticism, Dean Inge and Bertrand Russell; all I wish to suggest here is that one finds early indications of this. One of the last things Gruffydd wrote as editor of Y Llenor (xxx.1, pp. 1–2) had to do with a controversy that had arisen in Flintshire over the demand for a separate school for their children by Roman Catholics. There are dangers in summarizing, but Gruffydd in these notes is very critical of the Free Church Council for interfering in the disagreement. The Act of 1944 was operative and R.C. parents were within their rights in making their demands. If the answer of the local authority, who at the time were reluctant to comply, was that complying without delay gave the R.C. school an unfair priority in the building programme, then it was a difference of view on an administrative matter, not a religious dispute.

Many of my friends will doubtless be surprised to see me taking this standpoint and some of them will prophesy that before long I am going to follow Mr Saunders Lewis in to the Church of Rome. To answer these last-mentioned, may I say two things? First, I was never more firmly fixed in my faith in the principles of Protestantism, especially the section represented by the 'Independents', and secondly that our first duty, in view of the terrible state of the world and its rejection of moral values, is toleration of religious organisations which are different from our beliefs. If my fellow Protestants want a crusade, what about a great united movement to get the Church of Rome to co-operate with us against the Anti-Christ? It will be difficult and it will take time, and even if we fail, our attempt will be something positive and not negative like so many of our efforts in the past.

The concluding paragraph of these notes refers to the first thing Gruffydd ever published in the English press; this was an article in the CHRISTIAN WORLD in 1903, strongly opposing Lloyd George's campaign to persuade the Free Churches to be "passive resisters" against the Education Act of 1902. He goes on to explain why he disagreed so much with his fellow nonconformists over disestablishment: the main reason for this attitude was the conviction that the bitter strife was so damaging to the essence of religion.

After graduating he taught, but only for one year, in a school in Scarborough. He was glad to escape from the disaster by accepting a post in Beaumaris Grammar School. He applied unsuccessfully for an assistantship in English in the University College of North Wales, but his application in 1906 for an assistantship in Welsh in Cardiff was successful. The only biographical note that I can enter for the two years in Beaumaris is that he had some passionate love affairs; he told me long after, when all passion was spent, that he was very poetically in love in one of these affairs. The year 1906 is a milestone for another reason for in this year Jarvis and Foster published his CANEUON A CHERDDI. It is a hundred pages of text and includes the ode he submitted in the competition for the crown in the celebrated Bangor Eisteddfod of 1902, on the subject "Trystan ac Esyllt". The crown was won by Silyn Roberts and it will be sufficient to say that the distinction of this eisteddfod cannot be attributed to its successful crown poem; Gruffydd's poem was put second. This eisteddfod has become histori- cally important because of the chair winning *awdl* YMADAWIAD ARTHUR (*The Passing of Arthur*) by T. Gwynn Jones. In the special number of Y LLENOR brought out in honour and in memory of T. Gwynn Jones, Gruffydd in his chapter of

reminiscences writes of the friendship with Gwynn
Jones which came about at this time. As Gwynn
was during this period working as a journalist
in Caernarvon they were able to meet on free
days and walk and talk for hours.

I will do no more at this point than to remark
upon certain external features of the 1906 volume
of poetry. The introduction admits that extreme
youth cannot be used as a plea of defence and
there is an implication not only that this work is
more mature by five or six years than the earlier
publications, but that it is, apart from any
comparison, to be regarded as adult, to be
regarded as the work of a grown-up poet. It has
translations from Heine, exactly as if Heine were
a compulsory question in the examination
papers of the period. It has poems in sonnet form:
there is one poem in sonnet form in the earlier
jointly-published volume and this only deserves
special notice because Gruffydd used to believe
that he was a sort of pioneer in bringing the
sonnet form into use in Welsh. The table of
contents seems to indicate by means of a heavy
type that there are three poems of greater
importance than the rest and one of these is
AR YR ALLT which amounts to thirty-four
verses of the 'Omar Khayyam' structure. Morris-
Jones's CANIADAU was not published until a year
later (1907), with its translation of Omar Khayyam
and as I have no evidence that Gruffydd had seen
a draft of Morris-Jones's translation, I draw the
obvious conclusion that Gruffydd got his pattern
from Fitzgerald. Anyone making a selection of
Gruffydd's poetry would do exactly what
Gruffydd himself did in the Gregynog volume

and would choose the sonnet Y DDINAS, the lyric CREIGIAU PENMON, which because of its abandon and musicality is not really characteristic of Gruffydd's style, which normally is rather jagged like walking barefoot on rock and shingle; and would choose before everything else the group of four poems: THE SONG OF THE OLD CROFTER OF TYN-Y-MYNYDD, THE SONG OF THE OLD QUARRYMAN, THE SONG OF THE OLD SEAMAN, and THE SONG OF THE YOUNG POET. The first two have the provenance 'Llanddeiniolen 1902', the third and fourth 'Llanddeiniolen 1903'. The four poems, all short, are distillations of the lives and deaths of their subjects, wonderful examples of the definition that poetry is about essences. The poet who dies young is obviously a sort of Keats, the sensitive impressionable youth taking into the heart and brain the beauty that all five senses can experience. I pick on the second verse especially since it uses the word *llesmair* ('swoon') for it turns up again in the poem Y TLAWD HWN written in 1930, which is a poem of Gruffydd's own quintessence and expresses the ecstatic experience, caused by the intense beauty of sound or taste or smell that brings the brain close to faint or trance:

> *His soul loved to be afloat beyond the thunder*
> *He loved to hear the music of the spheres,*
> *And lovely to him also was to linger in the garden*
> *Midst the drug-like (or swooning) smell and sight*
> *of sweet flowers*

The implication plainly of the words *er hynny* ('however, nevertheless') is that the one whose thoughts dwelt on lofty matters, valued no less the immediate experience of the senses.

The other three of this group of poems have greater significance because they mark such a step forward towards maturity of thought and sympathy; and by thought and sympathy one means the intuitive power to interpret the forces and urges which have shaped the lives of simple folk. I think it is impossible to decide whether this faculty in Gruffydd's nature was stimulated by the influence of Hardy; I think it would be wrong to say that it was taken over from Hardy, as a sort of borrowing, but I am prepared to believe that the example of Hardy gave literary value and significance to peasant types, and gave the quality of poetic essence to the lives of simple folk. The crofter and his long day's work, with sickle clearing gorse, plough making straight furrow, getting corn to grow on the scanty hillside, and hardly ever resting from physical effort. He once knew in youth the joys of love before the skies of his life clouded over; and as he worked before darkness fell in his sloping fields he saw in his mind the face of the girl who had been long asleep under churchyard stone; He gave his hard-to-spare pence towards the building of the College; He gave his saddened life in devotion to the Son of the Cross; and the sunshine of two worlds shining upon his simple rustic heart Brought out the flowers of the two worlds during his lifetime; He liked to read the local newspaper from start to finish, But he preferred to hear told the stories of the past, He loved to hear in the sounds of the triple harp The echo of the songs of his far-off youth; Last night the sickle was hung up on a wall-hook;

He will walk no more over his strip of poor soil,
To cultivate the stone-filled land and sow seed
where the thorny bramble used to be.

This prose translation gives the "meaning" of
the poem; it cannot give the poetry of the
original, and one must rely on the ability of the
reader's imagination to recover what is missing,
especially the compassionate insight which sees
beauty and nobility in the very simplicity of this
uneventful, unimportant peasant existence.

The period of preparation is over and the first
chapter can be completed by giving the external
biographical events and incidents which provide
the outline of Gruffydd's literary life and activity.
There will be a great change in the tempo of
creative literary activity from now on: and one
reason, fairly obvious to us who know the size of
university teaching departments these days, was
that a young lecturer in Welsh, the only assistant
to the head of the department, did not have
much time to spare from teaching duties,
especially since Welsh as an academic subject was
so new and therefore lacking in texts and
anthologies and grammars and Gruffydd
belonged to the generation of university teachers
of Welsh who had to improvise and produce as
they went along these bare essentials of an
undergraduate course. One is not surprised
therefore that Gruffydd's next publication was an
edition of Goronwy Owen's CYWYDDAU,
published in 1907, and intended for use in sixth
forms and colleges. The next was Y FLODEU-
GERDD NEWYDD (*The New Anthology*), a selection of

medieval poetry intended as a college text book. One must not expect evidence of enormous, patient research in early works of this kind, to establish an accurate text and determine authorship; the scholarship of this kind of production is of the tip-and-run quality, and has not the slow-moving, test-match thoroughness of a later period. In 1909 Gruffydd married Gwenda Evans, the daughter of Thomas Evans, the Calvinistic Methodist minister of Abercarn. Mrs Gruffydd had been a student in Cardiff, and had graduated with honours in French. It is worth mentioning this not only because Mrs Gruffydd later published translations from French literature, such as the stories of Maupassant, but more important, this connexion supplemented the education Gruffydd himself had received in French, and made him far more familiar with French literature than he otherwise would have been. It is also worth explaining that Mrs Gruffydd's father was the Presbyterian minister of a flock which worshipped in a church, i.e. not in a chapel; it was a church built by Lady Llanover and given to the Anglican Church on condition that its services were in the Welsh language; if not, it was to be given to the Presbyterian Church of Wales, on the same conditions. This sidelight of history explains why in the Gregynog volume certain poems are denoted as 'Abercarn', and what must be puzzling to many, how Gruffydd sometimes used the address of 'Abercarn Rectory', for instance, at the end of the preface to the 1923 volume of poetry, Ynys yr Hud a Chaneuon Eraill.

The home after marriage was in Tongwynlais: the best known of all Gruffydd's poems, YWEN LLANDDEINIOLEN, has 'Tongwynlais 1909' as its provenance. If readers of Gruffydd's writings see references to the Squire of Greenmeadow, this was the name of the mansion and estate of the Lewis family, who were descendants of a cadet branch of the family of Lewis y Van. A mile to the north, and on the other side of the river Taff is the village of Gwaelod-y-garth; Gruffydd, as we say in Welsh, brought his letter (of member-ship) to the Congregational Church of Bethlehem, Gwaelod-y-garth, the minister of which was R. G. Berry. Although shy and diffident and unspectacular, Berry was a very remarkable man, possessing great literary gifts, as playwright, short-story writer and above all, as satirist and parodist; and yet more remarkable for his saintliness and preaching, which was far removed in style from the so-called *hwyl* but had instead a combination of scholarship, sincerity, earnestness and artistry. Gruffydd became greatly attached to Berry and had the same kind of respect for Berry as minister and preacher as he had for John Morris-Jones as scholar, or for Owen Edwards as educational and national reformer.

He won the crown poem competition in the National Eisteddfod held in London in 1910 on the set subject YR ARGLWYDD RHYS (*The Lord Rhys*), and another poetry competition with a dramatic lyric made to come from the lips of Goronwy Owen when leaving for the New World. Both are included in the 1923 volume, and although Gruffydd, if not contemptuous of eisteddfod poetry, was inclined to be deflatory even about his own eisteddfodic odes, these poems were given the author's approval for inclusion in the Gregynog volume. (Gruffydd does make out that his motive was to supplement his very slender salary as a young lecturer). The dramatic lyric is a fine piece of writing and makes poetry out of Goronwy's bitterness and *hiraeth*. The theme in the crown ode is the conflict in the mind of Lord Rhys, the prince of Deheubarth, whether to yield to Archbishop Baldwin's propaganda preaching and join in the Wars of the Crusades or remain at home to rid his own country of invaders. I don't think it is the function of a critic or interpreter to say how many marks it gets out of ten. It is right to say of both these poems that they show a very sure mastery and control of blank verse as a poetic form. Gruffydd had used blank verse in the 1902 eisteddfodic ode, and he used it again in shorter poems, such as GWLADYS RHYS (1921) and THOMAS MORGAN YR IRONMONGER (1922), CAPTEN HUWS YR ORIANA (1930); and it was one of Gruffydd's main achievements, I think, to make this poetic structure sound right in Welsh. It had been in use long before, of course, and there were others at this time capable of using it most effectively, such as Dyfnallt and Crwys. Blank verse had two different hazards, on the one hand the danger of being badly written prose and on the other hand, an excessive 'regularity', not so much because of a line-by-line structure, but because the accented syllables had too deliberate a down beat and because an unvaried positioning of the caesura gave a tee-rum-tee-tum rhythm, instead of speech rhythm, to the lines. Gruffydd had this mastery, I believe, because he had been fed on

Milton and Matthew Arnold and had the patterns or vague principle of their blank verse in his very being. One thing is perfectly obvious in the long eisteddfodic ode, namely the frequent use of the long contrived homeric simile; one is unavoidably conscious, whenever one comes upon them, of the 'standard' simile of epic and heroic verse in PARADISE LOST or SOHRAB AND RUSTUM.

Gruffydd published a very important paper in the TRANSACTIONS OF THE GUILD OF GRADUATES, 1907—1908 on "THE CONNECTION BETWEEN WELSH AND CONTINENTAL LITERATURE IN THE 14TH AND 15TH CENTURIES"; this was pioneering work and its value should not be forgotten merely because later scholarship has forged further ahead. Then there is another important paper on 'THE MABINOGION' in the TRANSACTIONS OF THE HONOURABLE SOCIETY OF CYMMRODORION, 1912–13, and a detailed bibliography would include various essays in the early WELSH REVIEW and other magazines. The reason for mentioning these things is that in a society and culture which rely almost entirely upon amateur and part-time authorship, the authorship employed in scholarship must compete with the scholar's urge to be a purely creative writer so that the gain of one sort of authorship is the other's loss. One might as well make the remark here as elsewhere, that Gruffydd's output of poetry after the 1910 eisteddfod, bearing in mind the amount of blossom in April and May, is really rather scanty; if one examines the dates of composition one sees how widely the poems are spaced and gets the impression of incidental, spasmodic authorship. Some second or third kind of authorship remained with Gruffydd throughout his life—scholarship, editorship, autobiography, biography, criticism, controversy—and poetry found it difficult to claim his attention. He wrote a play BEDDAU'R PROFFWYDI in 1912–13, which was first produced by the students' Welsh drama society in the Theatre Royal on March 12, 1913; the author himself taking a chief part. The drama as a form of art and entertainment was at that time in its infancy, and the inexperience and lack of technical skill in the tricks of the trade give an impression of clumsiness if one is conscious of the more sophisticated writing and construction of a later period. I often feel it was a pity Gruffydd did not persevere with playwriting and I also feel the same that he should have gone in seriously for story writing, but there is no point in pursuing these ifs.

A publication of his in the year 1915 was a translation of a pamphlet written by the very distinguished woman preacher, Dr A. Maude Royden. It is a pacifist sermon or address and the publication of the Welsh version was sponsored by the Fellowship of Reconciliation. This is mentioned to help understand the standpoint of the pamphlet. In the same year the translator joined the Royal Navy, in which he served until he was released at the end of the War. Instead of expressing shocked surprise at the inconsistency it would be far better to regard this as a typical 'horns of dilemma' situation on which Gruffydd's beliefs and behaviour landed him often. His attitude at all times was that of a religious pacifist; he poured his most vitriolic scorn upon the warmongering hypocritical lot, who got the cushy jobs at home and drove innocent youth with pious smarminess to mangled death and murder; the men who really stirred him into a state of eloquent admiration were the outstanding pacifists like Principal Thomas Rees of Bala-Bangor who suffered social ostracism and obloquy for his views; but Gruffydd could never be *absolute* enough to make the same stand himself. This was not fear or dislike of receiving a "white feather": it was his inability to take up an attitude of absolute conviction and taking all the consequential steps of this absoluteness. He could not reduce the issues involved in a war situation to a simple choice, as if one chose peace or chose to fight. One cannot go into all the complications of views and feelings, and this must be left but Gruffydd is not alone in this contradiction, of believing firmly that the Christian attitude should be that of reconciliation and peace but in spite of this intellectual or abstract conviction, admitting in a concrete situation of hostilities that one can't sustain this absolute attitude and yielding to the use of arms to defend all the other values of life and civilisation. Another aspect of this complicated attitude in a wartime situation was that Gruffydd bitterly opposed conscription, for this was violation by the state of individual freedom.

By the time he was released from the Navy he had been appointed to the chair of Welsh in Cardiff. I find it difficult to assess the relevance or importance of the information but I did hear more than once coming from students of the immediate post-war years the view that the malaria and dysentery from which Gruffydd suffered during the long spell of service in the Persian Gulf and in the Arabian and Egyptian deserts used to recur and make him extremely irritable and bad tempered and impatient. I can testify with first hand knowledge that he found the tedium of the desert countries and the boredom of the Red Sea really unbearable. The adjective which he applied to Egypt, *adwythig* ('deadly, baneful') remains in the minds of most of us associated with the opening lines of the poem Y FENDITH, written in Port Said in 1917:

> *As you are likely to return to Wales*
> *From this deadly-boring land.*

The few poems written during the war years have either a deeply religious feeling, pervaded with prayer for peace of mind and long suffering patience and compassion and the means of achieving true humility, or bitter satire, as if one of the sheep driven to the slaughter had turned around to butt and savage the drover. Anyhow, the public image of Gruffydd was formed in these post-war years, the man of the slashing utterances and violent criticism; and it may well be that the effects of malaria and dysentery turned out-spokenness into irascibility. We who are old enough to remember can well recall the 'public image' of prickliness and explosive outbursts; it may help others to be told that Sir Idris Bell, who was an extremely meek man, applied the words "enfant terrible" to Gruffydd; and the phrase does convey the impression of tantrums in some of Gruffydd's writing during these years.

In the spring of 1922 the first number of
Y LLENOR appeared. The quarterly journal Y
BEIRNIAD which John Morris-Jones had edited had
been discontinued. Now that life was getting
back to normal, there was obvious need for a
new literary quarterly to serve the needs of the
new intelligentsia, product of the university
colleges, liberated from the narrowness of
outlook and limited education of the preceding
generations, and bursting with superior
knowledge and an urge to be literary critics.
A meeting of representatives of the Welsh
literary societies of the university colleges was
summoned so as to bring a new journal into
being; the initial meeting, which made Gruffydd
editor of Y LLENOR was the only meeting. Gruffydd
carried on throughout the years, editing four
numbers every year, without reference to anyone,
except the Cardiff-based representative of the
publishers, Hughes and Son, Wrexham. It was a
most auspicious and fruitful period—and it
proved to be the most brilliant piece of literary
journalism in our history, for it caught the
authorship and scholarship and energy of the
literary revival and the enthusiasm of the new
enlightenment in full swing. All the great literary
figures of this marvellous period of authorship
published their poems and essays and stories in
Y LLENOR and it was the ambition of up and
coming writers to squeeze in somewhere amongst
them. No journal ever made such an impact on
Welsh life and letters. It was not difficult to make
a great success of editing Y LLENOR for it was like
harnessing the sustained flow of a great river and
making a hydro-electric scheme of it; but I must
not deprive Gruffydd of honour and credit for

his own authorship and prestige were such a very important part of the great volume of water. If one were to count up Gruffydd's contributions merely as a matter of wordage, the total would be very considerable and if one bears in mind that Gruffydd's intellect was really in its prime during the period 1922–39, and that he was now psychologically sustained by the awareness or even conviction that he possessed influence and enjoyed prestige, it is not difficult to accept and interpret the remark that he was the backbone of Y LLENOR; one should try to complete the metaphor by fitting the other contributors into position—R. T. Jenkins, Kate Roberts, Griffith John Williams, Saunders Lewis, R. G. Berry, T. H. Parry Williams, Iorwerth Peate, to name just a few. There was hardly a number without an article by the editor or review or poem or chapter of autobiography; and after the practice started of writing editorial notes, there must have been a special reason such as ill health to account for a number that did not open with editorial notes. These first appear in the first number of volume five (Spring 1926), and because these notes contributed so much to the character and reputation of Y LLENOR and go a long way to explain why it had such an impact, this first set of notes should be looked at; and in any case these notes are in themselves of great interest and value as pointers. The opening paragraph deals with the decision to publish editorial notes. The persuasion of many friends that it would be a good thing if he wrote editorials on general matters struck him as strange for whenever he had written on matters of public concern and interest he had caused offence or annoyance

to his fellow countrymen and put their backs up. The second paragraph lays down the principles of Y LLENOR's existence. It exists to serve Wales by helping to give it a literature that is worthy and worthwhile. What is the point of preserving the language if it is only good enough for haggling in a cattle mart or for chatting to old people, with the result that its speakers will turn to other languages in search of the delights and pleasures which great literature gives? The purpose of Y LLENOR is to promote and publish literary output of the highest quality and to provide an outlet for the true literary and artistic urge with no criterion other than intrinsic literary merit. Then comes a most interesting remark which draws attention to the change, which became noticeable the previous year, taking place in the political ideas of the younger generation of thinkers and writers. This has nothing to do with the transference of allegiance, from Lib. to Lab.; the reference is to the growing sympathy with the ideology of Reaction, resulting from a sense of disappointment with democracy, Saunders Lewis and Ambrose Bebb being quoted as examples. This Reaction has in it a great and passionate concern for the language and for traditional Welsh culture, but it also includes elements that appear strange in the Welsh context—a faith in and admiration of the socially superior classes, and a sympathetic attitude (to put it mildly) towards the Church of Rome. These young critics have a complete right to their views and they are fully justified in their criticism of Wales for attaching herself during the last fifty years to the English political system and for thinking in terms of this system. But why should we swallow the claims and pretensions of French political thinking? Here we find the first piece of evidence of the lack of sympathy between the minds and conditionings of W. J. G. and S. L., it was a constitutional or chemical incompatibility like acid and alkali; and although overtly there were expressions at times which the unsuspecting would regard as mutual understanding and admiration and co-operation, this incompatibility or lack of sympathy remained constant, deep down. The next paragraph of the editorial notes deals with the clamour for rejecting un-Welsh place names which had come into use and been officially recognised, and restoring the historically correct Welsh names. The editor's argument is full of common sense and moderation. Of course, monstrosities like Rhos-on-sea ought to receive disapproval; but the English are just as entitled to use Holyhead for Caergybi as the Welsh are entitled to use Rhydychen for Oxford. It would be wrong to spend any more time here over this particular editorial note but nothing could be more typical of Gruffydd than this kind of intervention and comment. The remaining paragraph expresses his concern for the well-being of the language, although ill-being would be the right word. There are many people filling important posts who got their appointments because they were Welsh-speaking or paid lip-service to the language, but who in actual fact are letting the language down, because the "teaching of Welsh" for which these are responsible as administrators or headmasters is just *camouflage*, and they ought to be exposed. Another class of people that get severe whipping are the leaders of the Church in Wales, that is, large numbers

46

of the clergy; for being so half-hearted or particularly disloyal to the language, and the evidence of this is that so many of them make no effort whatsoever to bring up their children to be Welsh-speaking, they manage to bring their children up to be uncontaminated with Welsh even in places which are overwhelmingly Welsh-speaking. If these editorial notes dealt with the need to reform the eisteddfod it could be said that the first series contained the seeds of the editorial harvests of subsequent numbers.

Professor Henry Lewis who became Gruffydd's first assistant lecturer describes how the book on medieval poetry (1300–1500) came to be published. Gruffydd 'borrowed' from the five students in the second-year honours class the notes they had made of his lectures, made his own copy of these and published them (after getting them into shape, presumably) as a series of weekly articles in Y BRYTHON the Welsh newspaper published in Liverpool, during 1921; and these became the book which appeared early in 1922. It is well to know this since a reader consulting it may possibly feel that the work lacks design and that it could not have been conceived as a single, unified structure. This is odd for when Gruffydd published anthologies he consciously set out to give design to the contents. When the series of volumes called CYFRES Y WERIN came to be published, (composed mainly of translations of foreign classics) Gruffydd's contribution was an anthology of *englynion,* the form of four-lined verse in strict metre and *cynghanedd* which in the modern period came to be used mainly for epigrammatic and

gnomic statements or definition of essence, not extending as a rule beyond a single verse. The compiler having made his selection makes no use of an obvious, external scheme or principle for his arrangement, such as an alphabetical or date of birth order, but devises a scheme of his own which relies largely on giving sequence to verses which are associated by their themes, and upon the order which is inherent in life itself, such as the seasons of the year, or birth and childhood and youth, leading to inevitable death and survival. After all, 'anthology' and the Welsh word made to translate it, mean "a collection of flowers of verse", and Gruffydd consciously intends the design to be not so much an enhancement of the poems, but a sort of artistry in its own right, like flower-arrangement, if one can think of this free from namby-pambyism. The other anthology, Y FLODEUGERDD GYMRAEG published in 1931, gave Gruffydd better scope as anthologist in the sense of this context. This is a collection of lyrical verse, the loose definition of 'lyric' allowing the editor to include eighteenth century hymns and twentieth-century sonnets, traditional verses sung to harp accompaniment, full of sparkle and wittiness and with folk-song simplicity, alongside weighty metaphysical blank-verse. There is much subtlety and insight in the design of this volume, and most of its readers have been prevented from appreciating the book as an anthology because they had to study it as an examination set-book, and spent more time swotting the introduction to get answers prepared than reading the poems for enjoyment and insight; and enjoyment and insight are not separate or even separable experiences.

To go back a little, a second volume of literary history and interpretation was published in 1926, dealing with the literary activity which took the form of prose between the years 1540–1660. This is a much more valuable contribution than the earlier book; it has not the odd derivation and composition of the first book and there are other differences. The scholarship and materials and ideas of a book appearing in 1920–21–22 are more or less those of 1914–15 and to use the *cliché* of our time, the breakthrough in the study and interpretation of medieval poetry came in the twenties and thirties, and that may be a sufficient description of the 1922 book. We had to go through the period of textual criticism first and then, when the several reliable texts had got into the texture of our minds, to adjust the lens of the twentieth-century in order to focus properly upon the medieval outlook and concern for form and formula and formalism. The 1922 book is somehow out of focus as a view of medieval poetry. The materials of the 1926 book did not require this change of focus, and are far more amenable to an intellectual interpretation, for they are the materials and ideas of prose and are nearer to us in time, of course.

In 1928 the University of Wales Press published Gruffydd's MATH VAB MATHONWY, a study of the origins and interpretation of the structure of the fourth story of "The Four Branches of the Mabinogi". This was intended for the scholars in Europe and America who were concerned with primitive myths and folklore and with the comparative study of early tales, and is therefore written in English. Those of us who were young students at the time were truly dazzled by Gruffydd's fertility of mind, by the originality of the ideas and the clarity of the exposition, but there were others who were not prepared to swallow some of his interpretations and a criticism of a later period is that he did not make sufficient use of the "comparative method". I mention another publication merely to indicate the industry or output of these years. This was a reprint, PERL MEWN ADFYD, of a translation published in 1595 from Miles Coverdale's A SPYRYTUELL AND MOOST PRECIOUS PEARLE . . ., which itself was a translation from a German original first published in 1548 in Zurich. It is an illustration of the policy of making texts available and Gruffydd was obviously attracted to the editing of the reprint because of the Welsh translator's connexion with Llanddeiniolen: Huw Lewys came from a home near Caernarvon and became rector of Llanddeiniolen.

The publication of the anthology in 1931, Y FLODEUGERDD GYMRAEG, has been referred to. In 1932 the volume CANIADAU W. J. GRUFFYDD came from the Gregynog Press; the number printed was four hundred. A brief note by the author states that several poems found in the earlier publications have been intentionally left out as they were the exercises of the apprenticeship period. Even in the case of the poems now reprinted they have certain things in them which now offend his canons of taste,

but I don't consider that a poet named W. J. Gruffydd producing poetry in 1931 has the right to alter the works of a poet of the same name who was producing poetry in 1910 or 1920.

This no doubt means what it says but the mode of expression has a characteristic mischievous, even wayward, twist, like the note in the volume Y Tro Olaf (1939) which thanks the editor of Y Llenor for permission to republish the essays.

Gruffydd first started to publish his "Old Memories" in the winter number of Y Llenor ix (1930) and the several chapters between 1930 and 1935 became a volume in 1936. A number of additional chapters were written and published in Y Llenor but without the regularity of the first sequence: it is intended to include these as well in the English version. If one examines the opening chapter one finds the inevitable Gruffyddian explanation of his motives for this form of authorship, the impulse which came in a moment of recall, a film of memory which brought back the sensation of his early life with such vividness and filled his whole being with intense happiness. Nothing could be more typically 'Gruffydd' or Wordsworthian. But there is obviously a sense of climacteric, an awareness that life is gradually slipping away, that one is now more inclined to look back, that one will never again experience the thrill and delight and wonderment of the growing years: these rich experiences must be preserved and the only way is to use the magic power of words to re-create the scenes and sensations of the past. This, obviously, is the real literary motive, that of protecting and preserving one's own life against time and oblivion, feeling that one's experience and view of life are too valuable to fade away, unrecorded and without trace. One must not expect this to be a process of pure reminiscing: the writer's mind has been trained to be analytical and critical and one must therefore expect his recounting to be narrative and interpretation and appraisal all together. I hope I am not overemphasizing the effect of this climacteric: one should not see a sudden change from light to dark, but from now on there is a growing tendency to be more and more identified with the generation of an earlier period, to feel removed in sympathy, away from the younger generation and to find good cause to defend the older generation when attacked by a newer lot, the very generation which he formerly wrote about with such virulence. This curve in the shape of one's life brings one back, not to the starting point but much closer to it than one had ever thought would happen, and further and further away from the top of the parabola. And Gruffydd, having regained this sympathy and thrown off the old harshness, is at his very best in these reminiscences; affection and kindliness of appreciation and understanding produce a living picture of the home and the chapel and the school, the parents and grandparents and the ministers, and people who would have been 'humbugs' or charlatans twenty years back, have now become 'characters' and possibly deserving of pity, instead of scorn. There could be no better example of this than the portrait of William Jones, M.P.

The first chapter of the biography of Owen M. Edwards was published in Y LLENOR VIII,1; 'trailer' would not be a well chosen word for the

year of the volume was 1937. It had been agreed
from the beginning with Sir Ifan ab Owen Edwards
that Gruffydd would write volume one, and that
the biography would be completed by R. T.
Jenkins. The preface mentions the first contact,
which was the first kindness, in 1899, and the
great help and encouragement he had received
from Owen Edwards and his wife throughout
the undergraduate years in Oxford.

*This volume is a sign that I think more highly of Owen
at this moment, in 1937, as a man and as a Welshman than
I even did in 1899; I have tried to give my reasons for this in
the book.*

It is an extremely well written book. It is far from
uncritical adulation or absurd hero-worship,
although naturally there is strong sympathy
since Gruffydd shared the point of view which
Owen Edwards' mission and educational policy
stood for and sought to achieve. It would be
entirely out of place even to give a summary of
Owen Edwards' career and views and achievements, but it is worth reminding ourselves that
his educational ideas were not pursuing the
same course as most of the authorities concerned
with Welsh education, central or local; and that
his desire to see education being far more Welsh
in spirit and language and purpose meant a
tussle with bodies and councils who did not have
this cultural awareness in their educational
policies, or in simple words, who were concerned
only to provide Welsh boys and girls with an
education for "getting on in the world" even if
it made them less Welsh. Gruffydd always
emphasised this conflict between Owen Edwards'

view and the educational system all around him; and one feels tempted to believe that Gruffydd took over from Owen Edwards this attitude of conflict with local educational authorities. There is one other matter which must be mentioned. Gruffydd was conscious that Owen Edwards had somehow gone out of favour with the leaders of the more politically minded nationalism. There was undoubtedly in the twenties a 'plugging' of Emrys ap Iwan as a source of Welsh national thinking and writing, a playing-up of Emrys ap Iwan and a playing-down of Owen Edwards, e.g. there is early evidence of this in Gruffydd's review of Saunders Lewis's pamphlet on Modern Welsh Literature (Y LLENOR V.4 pp. 197–8).

The volume Y TRO OLAF AC YSGRIFAU ERAILL published in the Spring of 1939 gets its name from an essay published in Y LLENOR XIV. 1V (pp. 223–231). The word '*light*' essay will not do, in case it suggests whimsical and shallow banter; on the other hand it is not like the other contents of the book which are a mixture of contentious or argumentative pieces and reviews and obituaries or tributes; it is a beautifully designed essay, profound and imaginative and moving, constructed out of the experience of cleaning and oiling and reassembling a grandfather clock. Gruffydd, by the way, was very knowledgeable about clocks and the mathematical theory of Time; anyhow, this was not theory; this was human experience, that as this kind of clock did not require any cleaning except once every twenty five years, it would be the last occasion for him to carry out the job; when the next time came around, it would be someone else's. This gives the theme of "The last occasion", and other experiences of this pattern are added, full of pathos, but free from sentimentality. It is the kind of writing which makes one say it was such a pity that more of it was not produced, and less of the passing and contentious and controversial. However, this theme has been described as an instance of the dominant thought of the passage of time and the transience of human existence and the mutability of all material things. During the course of my re-reading of Gruffydd's essays and reviews in Y LLENOR, I felt compelled to make a special note of his review (in XIII.2, 1934) of a book of letters written by an old sea captain to his nephew: it is so quintessentially Gruffydd to quote the passage which makes symbolical use of the voyage and the broker's yard:

Life is very much like a voyage, isn't it? And if an old sailor like myself were to jot down entries in his log on life's voyage, this would be the sort of thing set down. SETTING OUT: Breezes, gentle and free, sails full blown. The magic of the distant and strange shores strongly appealing. Seeing other ships on the voyage; talking to them and being told they are short of food. Handing over generously to them. THE MIDDLE PERIOD: Weather mixed and undependable, the ship finding it hard going. Food store getting low; signalling our distress to the ships that we had previously helped; on they go, paying no attention to our call . . . THE END OF THE VOYAGE: Consternation, strong currents and stormy; the ship, despite all efforts, gone off course. The sky clearing at last and the swell subsiding. And in light of day and calm sailing, making a true calculation to find my position, and righting myself by looking at the reliable steadfast objects.

Then after the long voyage, anchoring in Mortality Road, waiting for a tide that will take me to another sea . . .

The next phase is the most difficult to handle for it leads up to the by-election in 1943 in which Gruffydd stood as a liberal and is said to have stood in the way of Mr Saunders Lewis. One wants to avoid the unpleasantness of this old bitter experience which caused so much nastiness and bad feeling but it would be wrong to shirk it for although it does not look as if it were a 'literary' matter, in these affairs literature and politics and religious views and prejudices are mixed up, and there can be no possible doubt that the 'political' differences brought about a slump in Gruffydd's rating and prestige and influence in the eyes and esteem of the party whose aspirations he opposed and blocked. In fact he was never forgiven and as the world of Welsh literature came to be dominated largely by adherents of the newer school of political thought Gruffydd, one felt, came to be shunted off the main line into the sidings, and younger critics came to dismiss him as if he had ceased to have any relevance; as one who became president of the National Eisteddfod Council; who had become almost respectable, and whose criticism when he adjudicated in the Crown competition had turned into grumpiness.

I am running the risk of oversimplification, for the issues involved were extremely confused and most difficult to unravel, like a tangled length of nylon fishing line; but it is a risk that must be taken. Gruffydd was never very closely attached to any political party; he was most decidedly radical in the nineteenth century context, and he was on the side of 'reform' and he would certainly claim to be a believer in the democratic ideal;

and if asked what 'radical' and 'reform' really
meant, he would reply that it meant being in
favour of any change, in politics or religion, which
gave greater freedom to individuals to live and
develop, which lessened authority, especially
when it existed for its own sake. Gruffydd was
also very much concerned to protect Welsh
nationhood, the language and culture and the
institutions which made up a separate identity.
The political allegiances of most of us are com-
pounded of lots of principles and attachments
of this sort, but we have already picked up a bit
of evidence of a development which put Welsh
nationalism and a belief in an enlightened
democracy into conflict with each other.
Gruffydd feared early on that the leaders of the
younger generation were sympathetic to the
forces of reaction, the school of political thinking
which opposed the revolutionary ideal (in the
nineteenth century context) and the ideal of
setting man's mind free. Rightly or wrongly,
Gruffydd came to view this reaction as just a
manifestation of the authority and clericalism of
the Roman Catholic Church; and its political
expression later on was castor-oil Fascism and
the thuggish persecution of Nazism. It may have
been allergy or phobia of some sort, but Gruffydd
brought all these things together, they were all
of a piece, all those who suppressed freedom and
shackled men's minds, in Church and State.
Gruffydd came to belong to the Welsh Nationalist Party but he never got rid of the suspicion that
its leaders were 'right-wing' and reactionary in
sympathy and idiom, and too much inclined to
borrow ideas from Catholic and Fascist sources.
Because of this gnawing doubt and suspicion

he could never throw in his lot completely
with the W. N. P. He was truly aroused over the
"Bombing School" and by the meetings of
protest in Pwllheli; and later severely criticised
the move to transfer the celebrated trial from
Caernarvon to the Old Bailey. But one couldn't
be concerned only with the fate of Wales—I am
trying to interpret Gruffydd's position in the late
thirties; the fate of Wales, the Wales that mattered
to him, was in danger because Britain and the
whole of Europe were in danger of being sub-
merged under a tidal wave of barbarism. If it was
a question of priorities. Gruffydd had to put
resistance to the barbarism first for there would
not be (for him) a Wales worth preserving if this
barbarism were not resisted. One can go on and
on interpreting and reinterpreting. This attitude
resulted, in effect, in a drifting apart from the
leadership of the nationalist movement in Wales,
with bad feeling being engendered and nasty
things being said. There was an estrangement
long before the by-election. There is no space to
quote fully from the editorial notes of Y LLENOR
XX.4 (Winter, 1941): the main theme is the effect
of being conditioned by the values and principles
of one's formative years; there is an obverse side
that one is unfitted or made unfit to bear the
strains of a new set of circumstances in another
age. This is his way of explaining why he finds the
outlook created by the war so unbearable.

*I was conditioned by the optimism of the nineteenth century
and rendered unfit to make the effort to live in the ruins of old
aspirations.*

Gruffydd is here engulfed in gloom. He goes on to

58

deal with the damage done to Welsh life by recruitment and conscription and wartime transference of labour. It did not matter so much if somebody from Somerset was thrown into the company of others from Durham: his "english-ness" was hardly affected; the difference in the case of Welsh boys and girls was obvious. I mention these things to show what was upper-most in his mind; but I was coming to the next paragraph of these notes which speak of the bitterness and nastiness which have reappeared in the life of Wales—"Mae hen gyfeillion wedi mynd yn elynion"—"Old friends have become enemies".

The concluding paragraph is possibly more deserving of our notice:

All that I have written above is an explanation and an apology for my being a coward and a pessimist: it is not an attempt to depress others. I am not a pessimist concerning man's ultimate fate; I am completely certain about that, or, in case anyone may think that I am avoiding a statement of my belief, I will declare that I am quite firm in the most orthodox sort of faith concerning the ultimate salvation of man as the special object of God's love. But it makes a man a sorry wretch to see that the way which he believed in with such confidence in his youth is not the way chosen by Salvation, and what makes it worse still is to realize that this way is not coming through Wales. If Wales is lost, I at any rate have nothing more to say (or contribute) to life. Wales was my 'raison d'etre'; the life I have lived up till now, and everything I have written will be made pointless if there are no Welsh children living in Llanddeiniolen and Pont-rhyd-fendigaid and Llan-bryn-mair after I have gone into silence.

Gruffydd accepted the nomination of the Liberal
Party in the by-election in 1943 for the University
constituency and was elected; he was re-elected in
1945, and remained a member until University
seats were abolished. There is nothing in the
parliamentary record which is really relevant to
this study. Many of us at this period of life fall
prey to committee work; in fact Gruffydd had
always hankered after committee work, especially
in the University. There was less time for
scholarship and authorship, and the horrors of
the war years took a great deal out of him. He
also had a long period of poor health and
underwent a severe operation and even when the
war was over he found editing Y LLENOR
irksome. It had survived the war years by
changing from four robust numbers a year to
two anaemic so-called "double" numbers. Even
when things got back to normal the editor's
contributions were intermittent at best, and the
actual work of editing was carried out by an
assistant editor. When he retired from the chair
of Welsh in 1946 he moved to live in Chertsey, to
be nearer the House. He was beset by severe
illness again in 1948, and a serious operation.
When there was no further reason for living in
the London area he returned to Wales, and chose
to go to live outside Caernarvon, in a house whose
windows stared at Anglesey across the Menai
Straits. He took his "letter" back to the chapel
where he first became a church member and
regularly attended the services as long as his
physical condition made this possible. He died on
September 29, 1954 and was buried in the
graveyard of Llanddeiniolen, not far from the
yew tree of his most celebrated poem.

We may blame his involvement in non-literary matters for making the later period of his active life relatively unproductive. But a man who had written so much before this second climacteric would probably only repeat himself. A translation he made of the ANTIGONE for broadcasting was published by the University of Wales Press in 1950; a translation of KING LEAR was also broadcast. The one book of scholarship came from a series of lectures he was invited to give in Aberystwyth, these became the book bearing the title RHIANNON published by the University in 1953. Here are some of the ideas concerning the MABINOGI stories he had carried in his head but had never gone through the processes of detailed research and scholarly authorship. This volume has a valedictory character, a last will and testament, putting ideas down on paper, knowing that there would never be time and energy to research and elaborate, and recording them in case they would be lost for ever and might be of value.

Some attempt ought to be made in conclusion to make some kind of judgement on his work as a poet and creative writer, and his ideas and achievements as a literary figure. The great number and variety of his literary activities make it impossible to keep Gruffydd within the confines of a short essay; it has already been hinted that the poetic output was reduced because of the other interests and forms of authorship. Gruffydd might well have answered this criticism by insisting that the poet should not compose except on the rare occasions that the inspired mood had come upon him, or when he was in the world of the spirit, to translate a favourite phrase of his. But there can be little doubt that the concentrated 'professional' produces his own inspiration and it seems a fairly safe and obvious inference from the record that Gruffydd's activity as a poet came to be sporadic during the years of maturity and it has not the impact which the steady flow of the concentrated poet has.

It was characteristic of his formative period to make poetry a vehicle of social criticism and this suited Gruffydd's rebelliousness and the contrariness and 'odd-man-out' quality of his nature. His criticism and satire are meant to sting the society whose religion had become respectability and the acceptance of conventional external observance as a substitute for inner spirituality. One practice of Welsh non-conformity in particular gets satirised, and that was the way church membership was subject to a code of discipline, with the occasional 'trial' and expulsion, not so much for heretical beliefs, but for moral lapses. This system naturally is made out to be intolerant and lacking in compassion and forgiveness; the humbug gets away with it, the unlucky are made to suffer and become social outcasts. This hostility towards the self-righteous disciplinarians takes the form of compassion for the outsider and for anyone who does not conform with nonconformity: this idea pervades Gruffydd's work, his poetry, his satirical essays and play BEDDAU'R PROFFWYDI. SIONYN dies in a pub, of all places; the respectable raise their hands in horror; the satirist in his imagination sees Christ bending over the body of the old soak—"I have to carry you like every lame sheep". GWLADYS RHYS the minister's daughter is sick to death of chapel-chapel and is lured, poor thing, away from it all; she returns in sorry plight and is buried in the chapel graveyard: the minister as he walks past to enter the chapel does not allow himself even to glance down towards the grave; straight on, unbending, always in the right. The old ironmonger has been too busy in his shop to bother much about his immortal soul; he has had to be satisfied with an occasional free day and a call now and then in the local; all he wants is the chance to retire and go back to the company of sheepdog and other farm animals; his old friends in the pub may spare a thought for him when they pass the graveyard where he is buried; that will be his immortality, their memory of him. The crux of the play is the expulsion from chapel membership of a young man of great promise wrongly accused through a sort of frame-up. This makes an outcast of him and turns his life into a tragic failure; and the 'punch line' of the play is "If you had shown compassion". The poems and other forms of satire of the war years and immediate post-war years savagely attack representative figures of contemporary Welsh respectability, for instance, the kind of person caricatured in the poem called 'THE PHARISEE' or those who in the fervour of patriotism and holy war drove the young and innocent to the slaughter, or the profiteers who got into the honours list. Gruffydd at this period seemed to be working himself into a state of white-hot passion and indignation and there was a lot of this heat remaining when he wrote the introduction to the 1923 volume of poetry. Poetry should not lull readers to sleep; it should be a clarion to rouse feeling. This is the rebelliousness affecting his critical faculty, for judged even against his own poetry this is not a very relevant statement and has very little validity or soundness as a general statement about poetry. The poems that haven't this white-hot indignation are far better poetry. The tender compassion for Jonah Puw is on a much higher level, the old peasant who thought his life of slogging and suffering on this earth was utterly rewardless. Gruffydd "struck twelve", as we say, when this humanity in him, this large heart, made him draw compassionate portraits of simple souls and odd characters, sometimes with a smile of amusement mixed with the pity, the old ironmonger, the retired sea captain, the old fellow who used to come around the houses to sell tea, the old-fashioned tailor (in the essay Y TRO OLAF) who has made the last suit he will ever make, still waiting on the doorstep of his shop for a customer and waiting in vain.

Poems of this mood go much deeper than the scathing, seething, metrical lava. There is a still deeper penetration in the poems PLEADING WITH AUTUMN and the YEW TREE OF LLANDDEINIOLEN for there is a second layer of meaning: the meaning on the surface changes before one's eyes and reveals an inner or deeper significance. To take one of these, the "Yew Tree"; this monster yew tree, this ogre of the churchyard is looking and doing well because of the rich compost it gets; it makes exceptions of no one; big and small, rich and poor, they all end up here; all live under the depressing shade of this symbolical tree; in spite of this inevitability, young couples actually do their courting within the shadow of the very branches of mortality, they even laugh in the gloom, and one sees in the courting couple and hears in their laughter and indifference the first stirrings of procreation and the urge of Life in the larger sense overcoming what the yew tree stands for.

One could spend a great deal of time discussing the intuitive concept Gruffydd had of Life or the Living process; it recurs time and time again. I feel somewhat uncertain about the subject (for lack of knowledge) but the philosophical ideas of the late nineteenth century were trying to express in various forms the living essence and the process of living and perpetuating and changing and evolving and Gruffydd, it seems to me, had his own way of apprehending this. When I examined Gruffydd's writings on a previous occasion, I noted the frequency of this concept and quoted many instances. It was one way of judging things: were they on the side of Life or were they injurious; did they enrich or did they impoverish; if things smelt nice, it proved they were good for us; if the smell was horrible, it proved it was harmful to life; our instincts and biological laws were agreed (—and I am told they don't necessarily agree). But one finds little evidence of a firm belief in individual survival and old-fashioned immortality, a sort of endless extra-time after the game of life is over. The example quoted above of his conviction as to the ultimate destiny of man seems quite definitely to refer to humanity, to the race of man, inhabiting the earth. I may refer later to Gruffydd's quite open criticism of the Church (generally speaking) for misconceiving what its function should be and for laying its emphasis on the saving of souls, and neglecting, if anything, its more important duty of establishing the Kingdom of heaven on earth. If the words 'immortality' or 'eternity' or 'heaven' are used, I am sure they don't mean endlessness in time; they mean slipping out of the hold of time and normal awareness and experiencing a quality of existence which deserves to be called eternity or heaven, for lack of any proper vocabulary. I can testify from first-hand knowledge that Gruffydd regarded Y TLAWD HWN (1930) as his finest poem. The title is taken from Psalm 34, verse 6. *"This poor man cried and the Lord heard him and saved him out of all his troubles".* The poem does not get meaning directly from the psalm except the sense that the psalmist, the poor man, is not like the *others;* to quote the words of the synopsis: *"David praiseth God, and exhorteth others thereto by his experience".* The justification of the title is the sense of individualness of the poet, his separateness and his uniqueness, not seeking the heaven of others —or heaven in the sense of the delights of the multitude—but experiencing this through his imagination, fed by scholarship and beauty. It gets close to the meaning given to 'ecstasy' in mystical writing—to quote the dictionary definition, "the state of rapture in which the soul, liberated from the body, was engaged in the contemplation of divine things". There is in the closing lines an allusion to the "birds of Rhiannon" and "the sea of oblivion": this refers to the experience of those who returned from Ireland in the story of BRANWEN: although their seven-year feast is located in Harlech, and their long sojourn of eighty years is spent in an island on the Pembrokeshire coast, these places were origin-ally in the Celtic underworld or heaven; during the feast in Harlech, the seven survivors could hear the singing of the birds of Rhiannon far out over the sea but as distinct as if they were close by; and during the prolonged residence on the isle of Gwales, their grief and their sense of loss were forgotten, and in spite of the eighty years no one could tell by looking at each other that they were a day older than when they came.

In an extended treatment this poem because its meaning is so centrally important in Gruffydd's outlook would lead on to a discussion of the function of poetry. In sober and prosaic moods one would like to question the right of the imagination to visualise certain things, that is, "to make things up", for implied in Gruffydd's attitude (as a poet) is the supremacy of the imagination in its quest for beauty. This, I think, would be the poet's reply. The 'poor man' of the poem has a highly sensitive nature; he can't help hearing voices and promptings; he hears these expressions of beauty inside himself; he can't hear them for or on behalf of others; this beauty is an unshared experience, unavoidably subjective. In a period (i.e. in the late twenties and thirties) when there was an emphasis upon the social responsibility of the writer and the duty of the poet, as prophet, to be conscious of his duty towards society, to protect or lash or call to repentance, a contrast or polarity was made out to exist between subjective, individualist writing and 'social' literature, as if the subjective attitude implied neglecting or being indifferent to the needs of society, even in times of emergency. It would be a foolish oversimplification to say that Gruffydd, because of his attitude as a poet, was callously indifferent to the needs of his 'society', for his prose writing is entirely meant to have the motive of social service, but on the whole, this statement of the subjective nature of the creative experience does represent Gruffydd's point of view, as poet. He states more than once that he wrote a poem for his own pleasure, and in the introduction to the 1923 volume of poetry, this view, which is almost Calvinist, as to the special poetic gift, is set out with a force which strikes one as arrogant, and it is arrogant unless one remembers that Wales was teeming with bards or men with bardic names. There is a small number, indeed a tiny fraction of the whole, who are endowed with the sensitive apparatus of artistic perception together with the creative skill to transform the rare experience into words and music; these are the poets. There is a wider circle of people who possess a high degree of sensitiveness but lack the constructive skill: they have the taste which enables them to share the artist's pleasure. As to the vast majority even the angels cannot make them understand and appreciate.

To round off these observations about Gruffydd's creative work—one is made aware all the time of the difference between the generations, and this comes in all sorts of ways. The verses addressed by ' The parents to the child" (i.e. Gruffydd talking to his own young son) and written in a benign mood, have the three generations and the references to the child's grandfather and grand-mother are charged with reverence. There is another poem in which the generation that did the fighting of the First World War speak to the older generation; the mood here is bitter and biting. It is not merely these explicit examples that have this awareness of difference; the idea or the experience pervades Gruffydd's writing. It is the young rebel who attacks the complacency of the older generation, in regard to religion, or their blind faith in mountebank oratory in politics. This rebel is later made aware of new-comers and imperceptibly he comes around to have a far less impatient view of the older generation—and the lack of understanding of the newcomer generation impels him to defend and to vindicate the older generation.

No attempt was made above to make mention, as they appeared, of all the pieces of criticism—lengthy articles in Y LLENOR, broadcast lectures published in pamphlet form, reviews of a great variety of books, and of course, eisteddfodic adjudications, especially of the Crown Competition. Gruffydd did not have a systematic body of critical doctrine, or to put it clearly, he was not a systematist. In any case, his contempt for dogma and opposition to the dogmatic attitude would make him shun a system of doctrine for criticising and interpreting literature; and if he were called upon to justify a statement or vindicate himself, and to give the grounds on which a judgement was based, he would have to fall back on the claim (or admission) that he

possessed a critical faculty, that this had been
helped to develop by a wide acquaintance with
critical writing. There is nothing wrong in this,
I am just recording that Gruffydd did not belong
to a school of criticism, or have a fixed standpoint,
derived from religious or political belief, from
which to judge literature. He would regard this
as 'prejudice' and one often sees him made angry
or depressed by unfavourable criticism which
springs from prejudice, especially the criticisms
which deliberately set out to pay back an old
score, exactly like some of the theological
disputes of the nineteenth century. If he found
himself unable to deal with a book other than
by rejecting its contents out of hand, he preferred
not to show such 'confrontation': let me mention
one example and pass on; he could not review
Mr Saunders Lewis's book on Williams Pantcelyn;
when I once questioned him about it, he gave
this reason, adding that it was the most "wrong
headed" book ever written in Welsh.

Because he dealt with so many subjects in article
form there is an *ad hoc* quality about his criticism;
and one finds most acute observations and most
profound suggestions and bits of analysis scattered
all over the place in these articles and reviews
and published lectures. He was inclined to look
for the 'vision' which became an impulse
and source of creative energy. This would be
his method of accounting for the missionary
character of the work of Griffith Jones,
Llanddowror or Owen M. Edwards. One thing in
his style of exposition deserves mention: this was
the use of the illustration. Eben Fardd's first
eisteddfodic ode was a fine piece of work, the set

subject suited the descriptive style of which he was capable; when he tried to handle the subject of Job's tribulations, his descriptive style failed completely; and then when the next subjects gave him the opportunity to be descriptive he had lost his touch. The ship's carpenter of the old days used a sort of knife which was as delicate as a scalpel, it was ideally suited for the smooth and polished work required in the woodwork of the vessels. Suppose the ship's carpenter uses this scalpel to bring down a tree; he does eventually, after a lot of hacking, bring down the tree; the tree will be a poor specimen of tree felling; but what is worse is the condition of the knife; it has been ruined; it is no longer any good for the precision work for which it was first intended. Another celebrated illustration was used to help explain the way the intricate system of *cynghanedd* developed in our ancient poetry. The smith's original and proper function as an official of the primitive court was, amongst other things, to make arms including shields for the prince and his retinue. The shield would be a solid base of wood faced with a thick layer of metal to stand up to the fiercest blows from the clubs and swords of the enemy. The quality required in the shield would be its effectiveness in its actual use, its solid thickness of iron, able to resist shattering blows; it didn't matter if it was plain. In times of peace, there would not be any great urgency in the process of manufacturing the shield and more care could be taken over it, and if it was to hang on a post or a wall, it was a bit of decoration, not a piece of utility; it would become smaller and more and more ingenuity expended upon it, in the design and riveting and enamelling.

It will have been inferred from statements made earlier that Gruffydd, if the quest for beauty was a motive and an end, would certainly value artistry, and this was a word he frequently used. I have had occasion already to mention one thing in his class teaching, how he made out that there were two kinds of literature, the one that enriched living or added adornment to life, and the one that interpreted life; these of course could be fused in the same work; therefore one should not make a second inference, which would be wrong, that he greatly valued sweetness or subtlety, and ignored the penetrative or profound thought and feeling. And yet it is interesting to note, if I may use a wireless metaphor, how he jammed the 'message'. This is part of the conditioning of his generation, to react against the moralizing and didacticism of the preceding generation, and the use of poetry for moral uplift and telling little evangelistic stories with mawkish sentimentality. But this automatic opposition to the 'message' of poetry could go too far. For example, in the article in Y LLENOR, XIII. 4 (194—204) entitled "An Introduction to the Nineteenth Century", he describes or pokes fun at the mentality that concerned itself with the moral content of literature. He used to give a public lecture before the War on Dafydd ap Gwilym;

In order to make Dafydd acceptable to my listeners (ninety five per cent of whom, as in any mixed audience had no taste or gift to appreciate pure poetry) I had to interpret Dafydd's 'message', and it was that, the 'message' (bless my soul!) was a precursor or foretaste of the Protestant Reformation . . .

He later gives credit to John Morris-Jones for contributing greatly to the improved taste, by means of his public lectures. Morris-Jones had blind spots *"but he taught the nation to appreciate Rhobert ap Gwilym Ddu and Williams Pantycelyn"*. (Note—This is William Williams the great hymn writer and religious author of the Methodist revival in Wales): He was regarded by the nineteenth century as a hymn writer and reformer and "good man"; Sir John could condemn the century, without their knowing it, by emphasizing his greatness as a poet. When he used to declaim the hymns of Williams with such virtuosity, his listeners were the congregation made emotional by the Evan Roberts revival; but Sir John, in the intensity of his critical integrity, was really dealing with one who was brother to Dafydd ap Gwilym and Goronwy Owen. Like Paul on Areopagus, it was easier for him to preach his gospel through the mouth of "one of your own poets". This, I think, is an excellent example of the attempt to 'isolate' pure poetry; to read and enjoy the hymns of Pantcelyn as pure artistry, as one enjoys a lyric or a sonata, unaffected by the 'message'. We all know what Gruffydd is getting at, but we must admit that he is made to look absurd by this instance of isolating pure poetry.

This quotation serves one very useful purpose. It reminds us of one of Gruffydd's main contributions as critic and reviewer and adjudicator. We must praise him for exactly the same reason as he praises Sir John Morris-Jones, namely, for improving the general taste in literary matters, especially for raising the level of the appraisal of poetry. It was generally understood during his upbringing that the poem should walk hand in hand with the sermon as means of melting feelings and teaching moral lessons and telling young people how to be virtuous and how to get on. This led inevitably to sentimentality. It was also the peak period of that phase of our cultural development which made the practice of poetry so prevalent and common (due largely to the eisteddfod movement) and the great glut of verse resulted in a cheapening of the poetic commodity and an inability in the consumer public to distinguish between good and bad and atrocious. It was the denial of this assumption, namely that we were all bards, that brought out the bluntness, that only a very few had the true gift of poetry. It is not difficult to understand why a young student made familiar with the values and fashions then current in English literary circles, should question the right of so many in Wales to be bards. Essentially bound up with this questioning and denial was the rider, that the tear-jerking anecdotes put into verse form were sentimental trash, judged as poetry. If I may quote a word I have used on a previous occasion about Gruffydd's severity, his repeated criticism of the sentimental and the facile and the mere trickery of the lyrical trade had a wonderful antiseptic cleansing effect.

Gruffydd was always ready and willing to state what his views were on the great issues of belief and unbelief, and the fundamental questions of the philosophy of religion. It is not surprising that with his rebel nature he should welcome the chance which his academic training gave him to escape from the restricted views of his upbringing and to enjoy the freedom of thought and the sense that one could be free, not obliged to subscribe, and free to declare openly that one did not or could not swallow and had to reject. Agnosticism was in the air, modernism was the right attitude for intellectuals, if they remained within the confines of belief or church membership; there was a confident trusting of the scientific method and one should not panic and look for the shelter of a dark cave if the findings of scholarship made one's faith a bit shaky. It gets fairly close to the mark to say that Gruffydd's position or attitude was that of modernism and liberal humanism, which meant tolerance, a fair amount of scepticism and suspended judgement and the right of the human spirit to be free to explore and the human mind to enquire.

In a review of Keri Evans's "SPIRITUAL PILGRIMAGE" in Y LLENOR XVIII. 1, Gruffydd displays warmth of appreciation; but when a claim is made that God may enter man's life not only in abstract ideas entertained by the intellect but also through an intervention affecting the nervous system, the reviewer is completely unable to accept such a statement for it implies an interference with natural laws. The editor has an article in an early number of Y LLENOR entitled "Rebellion and Reaction" which in a way is a further instance of the consciousness of the divergence and the gap between generations. Those who are better acquainted than the writer with the history of ideas may be able to trace these concepts to earlier sources; it does not matter whether they are derived or original we are only concerned here to show that they contributed to Gruffydd's critical make-up. There is an urge in the young as if by nature to differ from the conventions and established modes of thought of the older generation and to feel a need to change the older system. This is a healthy sign, to struggle for change and to overcome the reluctance and resistance of the generation at present occupying the citadel. When the rebels become the custodians of the citadel they in turn develop a resistance to further change and the contest between these two urges is renewed. It is not necessary to say which urge gets Gruffydd's support. Some time after this he published an address which had been given to the Congregational Union, called "A LAYMAN'S IDEA OF THE CHURCH". The thesis of the address is that the Church, i.e. the really spiritual church, is the relatively small number of believers who are specially gifted so as to understand God's word and know his will. A distinction must be made between the Church and the World. The World is the bulk of mankind; the Church is the few metaphorically called the salt or the ferment or the light, and it was a grave error to think that the great unspiritual bulk should be penned inside *en masse* and called the Church. This summary probably makes strange reading and its brevity may be unfair to the argument; but it is decidedly not uncharacteristic of Gruffydd to have views of this kind.

A still more revealing statement of belief is the lengthy review of Principal D. Emrys Evans's short work on "Religion and Society". This is the review in which Gruffydd criticises the Church (as an institution) for its mistaken priorities; for thinking that it was an instrument for saving souls and failing to see that its duty was to establish the kingdom of heaven on earth. He firmly declares his adherence to "extreme Protestantism" as being the truly vital and healthy development of historical Christianity. The phrase "extreme Protestantism" is not the easiest standpoint to define; it means furthest away from dogma and primitive or superstitious belief, because it uses enquiry and scholarship to interpret and is therefore not static. One can see by a cross-reference how close this attitude is to typical rationalism. In the article which criticised the Presbyterian Church of Wales for expelling Tom Nefyn for failing to subscribe to a fixed creed, Gruffydd in his attack on dogma admits that he feels greater affinity with Bertrand Russell; and he uses Voltaire, Rousseau, Bentham and Mill "and other friends of freedom" as instances of secular minded thinkers doing far more that the officially religious to remove cruelty and oppression; and the only religious sect equally prominent in this respect, as if there were a correlation, are the least 'organised', namely the Quakers. To go back to the review, protestant denominations are as capable as any of stagnating once they get the upper hand and their protest becomes petrified, and the essence of true protestantism is continued development, away from the enslavement of the fixed creed, for this sort of change is a change towards greater freedom and therefore is for the good of the Life process. This implies that interpreting the mind of Christ is a continuing process, and that revelation moves forward, as a developing process. Gruffydd in several places deals with the nineteenth century faith in the inevitability of Progress and the concept of perfectability, and although these ideas were battered and pulverised by the calamities and follies of the twentieth century, he nevertheless sticks to the essence of this creed as a long-term principle. It may appear strange that even during the period of extreme pessimism of the Second World War he still clings to a belief in the ultimate outcome, that what is good and humane and benevolent will recover. This summary even as summary does not exhaust the philosophical writing of Gruffydd. Certain declarations of his have been briefly discussed as representative of his attitude and characteristic of his style and logic.

Not much needs to be said about the editing of Y Llenor; it did not need much editing in the sense of stimulating contributors even though there was no payment for contributions. The fecundity of the period brought in sufficient material with reasonable dependability, and as Welsh writers had known little about fees, absence of payment did not matter, and for most, it was sufficient reward to get one's contribution published in a quarterly of such high standing. When one speaks of editing, one is really thinking of the editor's notes, as they were called, and these played a large part in creating the personality of Y LLENOR (It would be wrong entirely to ignore the format, for until wartime shortages and regulations brought about 'utility' printing, it was a splendidly produced publication with its fine fount, wide margins, and paper of excellent texture). It was the editorial notes that made the existence of Y LLENOR known to people who were on the periphery of, or entirely outside, the circle of regular readers for the explosive nature of many of these notes caused rumbles and reverberations in other places, especially in the English dailies circulating in Wales. Just think of the talking that followed the notes on canvassing for teaching posts in the schools and the blunt comments on corruption and the mention of councillors being bribed, and the bad effects educationally of in-breeding in the way the teaching posts were invariably given to applicants of the appointing area and thereby to former pupils of the schools. Or the slashing criticism of the decision to buy the CODEX SINAITICUS—for the wrong reasons. One other example or topic must suffice. Gruffydd nagged and nagged at the National Eisteddfod to suggest reforms. Once the Eisteddfod had been allocated to a certain town, it became the entire responsibility of the local organisation to prepare the programme of events and competitions, and to appoint adjudicators and so on. The inexperience of the local organisers, completely new to the job and left unguided, led to incompetence, and the parochial nature of the organisation gave far too much room to local or even denominational considerations, say, in the choice of adjudicators or presidents, and in any case there was far too much English allowed in the conduct of the Eisteddfod proceedings. The notes, every time an opportunity came, attacked and criticised, and as the relations between the University and the Eisteddfod and the Gorsedd were very prickly for a long spell, Gruffydd would not be too particular when choosing his words and shaping his sentences. Reforms eventually were brought about with a new function of guidance given to the central authority of the Eisteddfod, and in the end Gruffydd himself was drawn into the Eisteddfod organisation.

I have tried to avoid giving an exaggerated or sensational view of a writer who certainly played a very prominent part in the literary life of the period 1920–1940, and around whom there was literary bustle. I am determined not to give judgement by making comparisons with others and to avoid superlatives. I think the best way of assessing him is to suggest that we make an anthology mentally, selecting examples of all sorts of authorship that came from him, poems, parodies, stories, literary essays, philosophical essays, literary criticism, book reviews, editorial notes, biography, autobiography, chapters of pure scholarship, and so on. A selection of the finest examples from all these categories would make up a wonderful volume, and present a writer of most varied gifts and accomplishments.

A Selected Bibliography

W. J. GRUFFYDD

TELYNEGION. (co-author with Silyn Roberts). Jarvis and Foster, 1900.

CANEUON A CHERDDI. Jarvis and Foster, 1906.

BEDDAU'R PROFFWYDI. Educational Publishing Co., 1913.

DYRCHAFIAD ARALL I GYMRO. Educational Publishing Co., 1914.

LLENYDDIAETH CYMRU 1450–1600. Brython Press, 1922.

YNYS YR HUD. Hughes a'i Fab, 1923.

LLENYDDIAETH CYMRU 1540–1660. Hughes a'i Fab, 1926.

MATH VAB MATHONWY. An inquiry into the origins and development of the fourth branch of the Mabinogi, with the text and a translation. University of Wales Press, 1928.

Y FLODEUGERDD GYMRAEG. University of Wales Press, 1931.

CANIADAU. Gregynog Press, 1932.

DAFYDD AP GWILYM. (St. David's Day Bilingual Book). University of Wales Press, 1935.

HEN ATGOFION. Gwasg Aberystwyth, 1936.

O. M. EDWARDS. Ab Owen, 1937.

Y MORYSIAID. (St. David's Day Bilingual Book). University of Wales Press, 1939.

CEIRIOG. BBC lecture, 1939.

Y TRO OLAF. Welsh Book Club, 1939.

ISLWYN. Memorial lecture, University of Wales Press, 1942.

ANTIGONE. (Sophocles). Translation. University of Wales Press, 1950.

RHIANNON. An inquiry into the first and third branches of the Mabinogi. University of Wales Press, 1953.

FOLKLORE AND MYTH IN THE MABINOGION. University of Wales Press, 1958.

CRITICAL

A critical essay by Alun Llywelyn-Williams appeared in Gwŷr Llen, edited by Aneirin Talfan Davies, Griffiths and Sons, London, 1948.

W. J. Gruffydd was editor of Y Llenor, published by Hughes a'i Fab, from 1922–1951. The memorial number to him, edited by T. J. Morgan, CYFROL GOFFA W. J. Gruffydd, containing articles by Ceridwen Gruffydd, H. Parry Jones, Henry Lewis, Stephen J. Williams, E. Lewis Evans, R. T. Jenkins, Iorwerth C. Peate, Cynan, Rhys Hopkin Morris and T. J. Morgan, was published in 1955.

The Author

Dr. T. J. Morgan studied at the Universities of Wales and Ireland. He taught for many years at the University College of Cardiff before becoming Registrar of the University of Wales. In 1961 he moved to his present position as professor of Welsh Language and Literature at the University College of Swansea. He is well known for his numerous writings in Welsh and in English on aspects of Welsh language and literature. His examination of the mutation system in Welsh is the standard work on the subject. He has published volumes of essays and poetry. He was closely associated with Professor W. J. Gruffydd for many years and for a period was co-editor of Y LLENOR. Professor Morgan is Chairman of the Literature Committee of the Welsh Arts Council.

This Edition,
designed by Jeff Clements,
is set in Monotype Spectrum 12 Didot on 13 point
and printed on Basingwerk Parchment by
Qualitex Printing Limited, Cardiff

It is limited to 750 copies of which this is

Copy No.

554